S0-AUC-848

TWELVE SERMONS
ON
VARIOUS SUBJECTS

TWELVE SERMONS
ON
VARIOUS SUBJECTS

C. H. Spurgeon

BAKER BOOK HOUSE
Grand Rapids, Michigan

Paperback edition
issued by Baker Book House

First printing, July 1974
Second printing, January 1976

ISBN: 0-8010-8029-0

PHOTOLITHOPRINTED BY CUSHING - MALLOY, INC.
ANN ARBOR, MICHIGAN, UNITED STATES OF AMERICA
1976

CONTENTS

"Even So, Father!"

" At that time Jesus answered and said, I thank thee, O Father, Lord of heaven and earth, because thou hast hid these things from the wise and prudent, and hast revealed them unto babes. Even so, Father, for so it seemed good in thy sight."—Matthew xi. 25, 26.

THAT is a singular way with which to commence a verse—"At that time Jesus answered." If you will look at the context you will not perceive that anybody had asked him a question, or that he was indeed in conversation with any human being. Yet it says, "Jesus answered and said, I thank thee, O Father." Now when a man answers, he answers a person who has been speaking to him. Who, then, had been speaking to him? Why his Father. Yet there is no record of it; which should just teach us that Christ had constant fellowship with his Father, and often did his Father silently speak into his ear. As we are in this world even as Christ was, let us catch this lesson. May we likewise have silent fellowship with the Father; so that often we may answer him. And when the world wotteth not to whom we speak, may we speak to God and respond to that secret voice which no other ear hath heard, while our own ear, opened by the Spirit of God, hath attended to it with joy. I like the Christian sometimes to find himself obliged to speak out, or if not to speak out to feel an almost irrepressible desire to say something though no one be near, because a thought has been brought to him by the Holy Spirit, a suggestion has been just cast into the midst of his soul by the Holy Ghost, and he answers to it. God hath spoken to him and he longs to speak to God—either to set to his seal that God is true in some matter of revelation, or to confess some sin of which the Spirit of God has convinced him, or to acknowledge some mercy which God's providence has given, or to express assent to some great truth which God the Holy Ghost has then opened to his understanding. Keep your hearts, my brethren, in such a state, that when God speaketh to you, you may be ready to answer, whatever troubles may ruffle you, or whatever trials may disturb you. Jesus Christ had just had a time of weeping, and it was succeeded by a season of grateful communion. Like him do you maintain an ear ready to listen to the voice of God, and at that time do you answer thankfully, and bless the Lord your God.

Now it seems to me, in looking through these two verses, that the Saviour would teach us three things. When we have learned these three things, I shall endeavour to turn them to practical account. He will have us first of all *seek after an enlightened apprehension of the character of God as Father, and yet Lord of heaven and earth.* He would have us next observe carefully, *the manifest discrimination of his grace*—"Thou hast hid these things from the wise and prudent, and hast revealed them unto babes." He would have us, thirdly, *cultivate a spirit entirely in harmony with the divine will,* thanking him that he hath done all things according to his own purpose—"Even so, Father, for so it seemed good in thy sight."

I. First of all, then, THE SAVIOUR WOULD HAVE US ATTAIN TO AN ENLIGHTENED APPREHENSION OF THE CHARACTER OF GOD.

Concerning the character of God, what gross mistakes men make! I believe it is a mistake about God himself which has been the root and foundation of all the mistakes in theology. Our conviction is, that Arminian theology, to a great extent, makes God to be less than he is. The professors of that system have come to receive its doctrines, because they have not a clear understanding either of the omnipotence, the immutability, or the sovereignty of God. They seem always to put the question, "What ought God to do to man who is his creature?" We hold that that is a question that is never to be put, for it infringes the sovereignty of God, who has absolute right to do just as he wills. They ask the question, "What will God do with his promises, if man change his habit or his life?" We consider that to be a question not to be put. Whatever man doeth, God remaineth the same and abideth faithful, though even we should not believe him. They put the question, "What will be done for men who resist God's grace, if in the struggle man's will should be triumphant over the mercy of God?" We never put that question: we think it blasphemous. We believe God to be omnipotent, and when he comes to strive with the soul of man, none can stay his hand. He breaks the iron sinew, and dashes the adamantine heart to shivers, and ruleth in the heart of man as surely as in the army of the skies. A right clear apprehension of the character of God we believe would put an end to the Arminian mistake. We think, too, that ultra-calvinism, which goes vastly beyond what the authoritative teaching of Christ, or the enlightened ministry of Calvin could warrant, gets some of its support from a wrong view of God. To the ultra-calvinist his absolute sovereignty is delightfully conspicuous. He is awe-stricken with the great and glorious attributes of the Most High. His omnipotence appals him, and his sovereignty astonishes him, and he at once submits as if by a stern necessity to the will of God. He, however, too much forgets, that God is love. He does not make prominent enough the benevolent character of the Divine Being. He annuls to some extent the fact, that while God is not amenable to anything external from himself, yet his own attributes are so blessedly in harmony, that his sovereignty never inflicted a punishment which was not just, nor did it even bestow a mercy until justice had first been satisfied. To see the holiness, the love, the justice, the faithfulness, the immutability, the omnipotence, and the sovereignty of God, all shining like a bright corona of eternal and ineffable light, this has never been given perfectly to any human being, and inasmuch as we have not seen all these, as we hope yet to see them, our faulty vision has been the ground of divers mistakes. Hence hath arisen many of the heresies which vex the Church of Christ.

Now, my brethren, I would have you this morning look at the way in which our Lord Jesus Christ regards God :—" Father, Lord of heaven and earth." If you and I cannot know the Almighty to perfection, because of *His* greatness and of *our* shallow · ness, nevertheless let us try to apprehend these two claims upon our adoration, in which we owe to God the reverence of children, and the homage of subjects. Father!—Oh what a precious word is that! Here is authority. "If I be a father where is mine honour?" If ye be sons where is your obedience? But here is affection mingled with authority, an authority which does not provoke rebellion, an obedience demanded which is most cheerfully rendered—which would not be withheld even if it might. Father!—Here is a kingly attribute so sweetly veiled in love that the king's crown is forgotten in the king's face, and his sceptre becomes not a rod of iron, but a silver sceptre of mercy—the sceptre indeed seems to be forgotten in the tender hand of him that wields it. Father!—Here is honour and affectionateness. What are a father's bowels to his children? That which friendship cannot do, and mere benevolence will not attempt to do, a father's heart and hand must do. They are his offspring, he must bless them ; they are his children, they spring from his own loins—he must show himself strong in their defence. Oh get that thought of God, that while you obey him as Father, yet you love him as Father ! Do not go about the service of God as slaves about the taskmaster's toil, but run in the way of his commands because it is your Father's way. Yield your- selves up to be the instruments of righteousness, because righteousness is your father's will, and his will is the will of his child. In a father, then, you will observe there is mingled authority with affection, and there is also mingled origination with relation ship. The man is not father to everything he produces. He may make the vessel, he may spend much skill upon it as he turns it upon the wheel, but he is not its father. Even so God made the stars, but he is not their father. He made the very angels, but I wot not that he said unto them at any time, "Ye are my sons." It is true in the sense of origination we are all his offspring, for he made us all. But oh !

again let me repeat the sweet word—Father! Father! There is relationship here as well as origination. We are like him that made us—we, his chosen, are the next of kin to the King of kings, his children; then heirs; heirs of God, and joint heirs with Christ Jesus,—a relationship which never can be dissolved. A child can never be anything but the son of his own father,—a relationship which no sin can ever break, and no pains can ever loosen. The father is a father still, though his child be draggled in the mire, although he spit in his very father's face. The relationship is not to be removed by any act either of father or of son. So stands it with the people of God. They are not only his creatures, but doubly his creatures, for he hath created them anew in Christ Jesus; they have a relationship, for they are partakers of the divine nature, having escaped the corruption which is in the world through lust. They are so near to him that none can stand between the sons of God and God their Father, save Jesus Christ the only begotten Son, who is the link of union between the twain. Father! He that can lisp that word upon his knees has uttered more eloquence than Demosthenes or Cicero ever knew. Abba, Father! He that can say that, hath uttered better music than cherubim or seraphim can reach. Abba, Father! There is heaven in the depth of that word! Father! There is all I need; all I can ask; all my necessities can demand; all my wishes can contrive. I have all in all to all eternity when I can say "Father." Oh! do not, I pray you, look upon God as a great King, unless you can also regard him as your Father. Do not dare to come into the intense brightness of his sovereignty, for it will be to you thick darkness unless you can call him Father. While you stand amazed at him, dare not to look at the sun till you have the eagle eye of the spirit of adoption lest it blind you. Launch not upon the sea of sovereignty till you have Fatherhood to stand at the helm, but then your little vessel may go from the shallows to the great deeps, and the deeper the sea shall be, the farther shall you be from the rocks, and the higher shall you be lifted above the quicksand. You may go as far as you like in believing him to be Lord of heaven and earth, if you can first recognise him as being Father to your soul.

Permit me here, however, to remark that many Christians are effeminate in their theology. They are weak in their faith, because while they can say "Father," they do not ✳ acknowledge God as being Lord of heaven and earth. I take it that Jesus meant by this expression that the Father was by power and by right Lord of heaven and earth. We all concede that he is Lord of heaven and earth by power. From the dazzling wing of the angel down to the painted wing of the fly, all flights of beings are controlled by him. From the roar of earth's direst convulsions down to the gentle falling of a rain-drop, all sounds that break on mortal ears are modulated by him. From the flash of lightning down to the glimmer of the glow-worm's lamp, there is no light or spark that his power doth not kindle. He doeth as he wills. Fools see men doing, wise men discern God doing all. In the loftiest emperor we see Jehovah's tool and nothing more. In the mightiest patriot we see but an instrument in the hand of God. In all that man hath done, whether it be perverse or excellent, we have learned to look beyond the material agents, and while we award to one execration and to another honour, yet we see God working all things after the counsels of his will. I am verily persuaded that the wildest fury of the storm is ordered in the eye of God; that he hath a bit in the mouth of the tempest to rein in the winds. And so it is when battle is let loose, and war rageth abroad, and nations are broken as with a rod of iron, as though they were but potters' vessels. In every catastrophe and calamity there is the reigning God, stalking victorious over the battle-field to whichever side triumph may turn; walking among cabinets and making their folly serve his wisdom; entering the heart of man, and making its very stubbornness the pliant slave of his superior might. He ruleth everywhere by power.

There are some Christians who, not knowingly perhaps, but unwittingly, discountenance the fact that Jehovah is Lord of heaven and earth by right. Brethren, I pray you learn this. You have not the key of a solid theology till you know this. Great God thou hast absolute right to do whatever thou wilt with thine own creatures, and especially since man hath fallen thou hast a right utterly to destroy him or to save him as seemeth good in thy sight. No man has any right to anything from God. Whatever right he had as a creature he forfeited when he sinned. Now God declares, and we acknowledge it to be a declaration of unimpeachable right—"I will have mercy on whom I will have mercy. I will have compassion on whom I will have compassion"—"So, then, it is not of him that willeth nor of him that runneth, but of God that showeth mercy. What if God, willing to shew his wrath and to make his power known, endured with much long-suffering the vessels of wrath fitted to destruction,

9

and that he might make known the riches of his glory on the vessels of mercy, which he had afore prepared unto glory." Who shall find fault, or who shall dispute his will? I would that the Christian Church did not cavil at God's sovereignty. I grant you it is an awful doctrine. All great truths must produce awe upon little minds like ours. I grant you it is a doctrine which the boasted freedom of man's thoughts will not readily receive. Be it so; it is the more true to me; for what is this freedom of men's thoughts in modern times but licentiousness? What is it but a sort of mental dissoluteness by which they say, "We will cast off the yoke of God; we will break his bands in sunder, and cast away his cords from us?" Oh! be wise. Kiss the Son for he is your King; bow down before your God, for dispute it as ye may, he is your Lord. Yield to his sovereignty, for he will be sovereign, even if you will not meekly yield. Confess that he has a right to do as he wills, for he will do as he wills whether you confess it or no. Do not seek to deny his right to reign, but rather say, "The Lord reigneth, let the earth rejoice; let the multitudes of the isles be glad thereat." Where could power be better placed—who better could be trusted with all strength than the infinitely wise, the boundlessly good? Great God! It were a calamity indeed if thou hadst not an absolute right to do thine own will, when that will is always good, and always right, and always kind, and always best for the sons of men.

II. Well now, brethren, if you have got a clear and enlightened apprehension of God's relationship as Father, and yet as Sovereign Lord, I am not afraid to trust you with the study of doctrine; you will not go far wrong. But next, Christ would have us carefully observe THE DISCRIMINATING CHARACTER OF GOD'S GRACE. "Thou hast hid these things from the wise and prudent, and hast revealed them unto babes."

Is it not, my dear friends, a notorious fact that the things of God are hidden from the wise and prudent? Cast your eye around now upon the great men in the literature of to-day—how very few of them are willing to receive the things of God! And though in the past we can number among reasoners such men as Locke and Bacon, and among poetic minds such men as Cowper and as Milton,—though we can go back and find some men of wisdom, and some men of great mental calibre, who have received the truth as it is in Jesus,—yet still it is to be confessed that they make but a very small part of the great whole. They are but the exception which proves the rule. It is true of ancient and modern, the past and the present,—"These things are hidden from the wise and prudent." See what the wise and prudent do. A large number of them will disdain to listen to the things of God. "Pooh!" say they, "religion for the mob; it suits very well the poor, we dare say, but we are intelligent, we are instructed; we do not need to go and hear such mere simplicities and elementary teaching as that." So they turn upon their heel and go and speak against the thing which they have never heard, or which, if they have heard, they have not understood. Then those who will hear—do you not perceive how they cavil? Where the poor simple-minded man walks right straight into heaven's gate, these men have raised objections to the manner in which the nails are put in the gate, or to certain stones that pave the way; and they cannot go in until they know the precise pattern of everything in the heavenly place. They raise objections where we should see none. While we take the provisions of truth, and sit down and feed at the table, they are objecting to the way in which the flesh is carved or the wine poured out. And then there are others of them who not only raise objections, but set themselves wilfully to oppose. Mark you this; I do not believe there is a single honest man living who, having once heard the gospel simply preached, does not in his conscience believe it to be true. I am persuaded that light will penetrate. There is such force, such energy in Christ—the power of God and the wisdom of God—it must and will pierce through some crevice, and convince at least a natural conscience. But this is the very reason why men oppose it: they do not want it to be true. It would be unpleasant for them if it were true. They would be compelled to live more strictly than they do. They feel it would cut against their previous notions, and pull down their old prejudice. They love darkness. What they do not want to be true they try to prove not to be true, and that is the easiest thing in the world. I could prove by syllogism any lie which I wanted to believe, and so could you. You can either bid the truth be quiet because its shrill note awakes you out of a sleep which you love, or else you can set up a counter-noise which shall drown the unwelcome sound, so that you cannot hear the celestial voice. I know why men brag; we well understand why they speak loud words of blasphemy. As sure as ever a man is too bold, there is an unquiet conscience to prompt him. Do not set down the blasphemies of Voltaire to any real doubts; that man was as firm a believer as you and I, but he was not honest. Do not put down, I pray you, the blatant blasphemy of Tom Paine to a conviction that Christianity was not true. He knew it was true, and he, perhaps, of all men was the grossest of liars to his own soul, for he fought against a truth which his own conscience acknowledged to be taught of God. Oh! let us see to it that while these wise and prudent men are discussing, and disputing, and objecting, and dividing, let us see to it that we do not imitate them, lest haply these things should be hidden from us, and not revealed to us though we are babes.

But while these wise and prudent ones are passed by, how graciously God has revealed his truth to babes, to men of simple minds! In the eye of the wise they might be credulous; in the judgment of the prudent they might be superstitious; but they heard the gospel; it fitted their case; it was just the thing they wanted; they were guilty, it offered them pardon; they were lost, it provided them a Saviour; they were cast away, it found them a Shepherd who had come to seek and to save that which was lost. They took it; they laid hold of it; they found it gave them joy and comfort, peace and rest. They went on; they found their experience tallied with what they had learned. They examined more and more. They never found a flaw or discrepancy between the feelings within and the teaching without. And they, though they were but babes, and could not argue, though they were but children and could not discuss, though they were fools and did not pretend to be wise,— they entered into the kingdom of God, and attained to the enjoyment of the peace which Jesus gives to them that trust him.

Do you ask why is it God has not been pleased to call by his grace the wise and prudent? Albert Barnes says, as a reason why the wise and prudent do not come, "Because they have peculiar mental temptations; because they think the gospel to be beneath their consideration; because it does not flatter their pride; and because, again, they are so occupied with their wisdom that they have no time for the things of God." Now these are very good reasons why they do not accept the gospel, but not the reason why God does not call them. God's reason for calling or not calling a man is not in man but in himself. So we are told in the text—"Even so, Father, for so it seemed good in thy sight." Why, then, did he not call them? You may ask Gabriel before the throne, but he cannot tell you; you may ask all the people of God everywhere, but they cannot tell you either; for the reason is, that God willed it, and there we must let it rest. "Even so, Father, for so it seemed good in thy sight." He could have converted emperors upon their thrones; he could have made the philosopher a preacher; he could, if he would, have subdued the loftiest mind to his service. If he rather then chose the fishermen and the unenlightened peasants of the Lake of Galilee, he did so because he would. There we must leave it; ask no account of his affairs, but tremble and be still.

III. Yet when we come to our last point, which we shall now do, I think we shall see some reason why we can in our very hearts most truly acquiesce, and admire the wisdom and graciousness of the divine choice. I come, then, to this third point, THE SAVIOUR WOULD HAVE HIS PEOPLES' HEARTS IN PERFECT AGREEMENT WITH THE WILL AND ACTION OF GOD. "Father," said he, "I thank thee that thou hast hid these things from the wise and prudent, and hast revealed them unto babes."

Brothers and sisters, can you say, "I thank thee, Father," too? Many of you can for personal reasons, for you were babes. Ah, we were each of us but babes. He who stands before you, if he be chosen of God, as he trusts he is, certainly never belonged to the wise and prudent. When I have sometimes had it flung in my teeth—"This man was never educated at college; this man came into the ministry in literary attainments totally unprepared for it; he is only fit to address the poor; his ministry is not polite and polished; he has but little classical instruction; he cannot read forty languages;" I say, Precisely so; every word of it is true, and a great deal more. I would not stay you; if you will go on, if you will just show me more my folly, if you will just discover to me yet more my want of prudence, if the wise man would say, "This man takes a daring project in hand and does not consult any man, does not ask anybody about it, but goes and does it like a madman,"—just so; precisely so; I will agree to the whole of it; but when I have said this I will remind you that "God hath chosen the base things of this world to confound the mighty, and the things that are not. to bring to nought the things that are." On this wise I will put it, in this thing I will become a fool in glorying,—What have your college men done that is comparable to this work? What have the wisest and most instructed of modern ministers done in the conversion of souls compared with the work of the unlettered boy? It was God's work, and God chose the most unfitting instrument that he might have the more glory.

And he shall have the glory—I will not take any of it myself by pretending to an education I have not received, or an attainment I do not possess, or an eloquence which I never coveted. I speak God's words, and God, I know, speaks through me and works through me, and unto him be the glory of it. I can join with many of you personally for thanking him that he has "revealed these things to babes, which have been hidden from the wise and prudent;" but perceive you not, my brethren, that if the Lord in his sovereignty had taken another course, it would have been our duty still to be thankful? Yet we should have lacked one reason for joy which we have to-day; it is this:—God, in the choice of the base things of this world, has manifestly cast a slight upon all human glorying. Ah! ye that boast your pedigrees! He has dashed them. Ye that flaunt your golden eagles—ye lack the splendour of his smile. Ye who are clothed in purple, and ye who fare sumptuously every day—what careth he for your greatness? Let the crowd stand and gape at you, let the fool bow down in admiration, but the King of kings, the Lord of lords, regardeth you no more than menials that serve his will, but are not of his council, and know not his secret. He hath put a stain upon proud distinctions. See, too, how he spits upon the boastfulness of human learning! And ye that have the key of heaven, and will not enter yourselves, neither suffer the poor and ignorant to enter—how hath he laughed at your pretensions! "The scribes and Pharisees sit in Moses' seat and they say, 'We are the men, and wisdom will die with us.'" They come forth, flaunting their degrees and boasting their high and lofty erudition, but he casteth dust into your faces, and leaveth you all to your blind confusion. Then, stooping down from his mightiness, he taketh up the babe. Though it be a learned babe, if it be a babe, he taketh it. I mean, though it hath riches, though it hath skill, though it hath erudition, he doth not cast it away from him for that reason, but he doth not choose it for that reason either. He takes it; it is a babe; it is willing to be nothing; it is willing to be a fool. The prince may be as willing to be saved as the pauper is; the great man may be willing to stoop and to lie at the feet of Jesus as though he were nobody. He takes these; these are the men that God hath chosen—humble and contrite—they that tremble at his Word. Oh! because he has thus stained the pride of all glory, let his people rejoice; let all his saints be glad thereat!

I wish, my dear friends, that those who are so afraid of the doctrine of election, would remember that it is the only lasting source of joy to a Christian. You say "How is that? Surely we ought to rejoice most in our usefulness." No, no. The twelve apostles went out to preach, and they were so successful that Christ said, "I saw Satan as lightning fall from heaven," but he said to them, "Nevertheless, rejoice not in this, but rather rejoice because your names are written in heaven." Our election is a perennial spring. When other streams are dry, the fact that our names are written in heaven shall yield us comfort still. And you will remark, as I have before observed, Christ had just been exceedingly sorrowful because Capernaum and Bethsaida had rejected his Word, but he finds comfort, and begins to thank his God because there was a remnant after all, according to the election of grace. People of God! do not stand afraid of this precious truth, but love it, feed upon it, rejoice in it, and it shall be as oil to your bones, it shall supply them with marrow, and give strength to your very being.

IV. Having thus explained the text as best I could, I want your earnest attention while I try to make some practical use of it. Three or four things to three or four characters.

A word to those Christians who are downcast, trodden, afflicted. You have lost a friend; you have had crosses in your business; you have been tried in body, you have been afflicted by the calumnies of your enemies. Very well; but you have still something to rejoice about. Come, dry those eyes; take that harp from the willow. Come, now, sit no longer on the dunghill; take off that sackcloth, remove those ashes; take the oil of joy, and put on the garment of praise, and say this morning, "Father, I thank thee that thou hast hid these things from the wise and prudent, and hast revealed them unto babes." At least, you have this to thank God for—although you were a simpleton, a very fool in your own estimation, yet you have received the truth as it is in Jesus, and you have been saved thereby. Let all the chosen seed be glad, and take heart and rejoice in God.

The next piece of practical instruction is this: let us learn, my brethren, the wicked folly of those professed Christians who despise the poor. There is growing up, even in our Dissenting Churches, an evil which I greatly deplore—a despising of the poor. I frequently hear in conversation such remarks as this, "Oh, it is no use trying in such a place as this, you could never raise a self-supporting cause. There are none but poor living in the neighbourhood." If there is a site to be chosen for a chapel, it is said, "Well, there is such a lot of poor people round about, you would never be able to keep a minister. It is no use trying. They are all poor." You know that in the City of London itself, there is now scarce a Dissenting place of worship. The reason for giving most of them up and moving them into the suburbs, is that all the respectable people live out of town, and of course, they are the people to look after. They will not stop in London, they will go out and take villas, and live in the suburbs ; and therefore, the best thing is to take the endowment which belonged to the old chapel, and go and build a new chapel somewhere in the suburbs where it may be maintained" "No doubt," it is said, "the poor ought to be looked after, but we had better leave them to another order, an inferior order,—the City Missionaries will do for them—send them a few street preachers." But as to the idea of raising a cause where they are all poor people, why there is hardly a minister that would attempt it. Now, my experience of poor people teaches me that all this talk is folly. If there be any people who love the cause of God better than others, I believe it is the poor, when the grace of God takes real possession of their heart. In this place, as an instance. I believe we have but very few who could be put down among the rich. There have been some who have cast in their lot amongst us just now, but still the mass who did the work of building this house, and who have stood side by side with me in the battle of the last seven years, must be reckoned among the poor of this world. They have been a peaceable people, a happy people, a working people, a plain people, and I say, "God bless the poor !" I would fear no difficulties whatever in commencing a cause of Christ, even though the mass were poor ; for I am persuaded that the rich who are truly the people of God, love to come and assist where there are poor. If you were to cast out the poor, you cast out the Church's strength, you give up that which is after all, the backbone of the Church of Christ. I think we have been doing wrongly in neglecting the City of London itself. It is true, I do not believe some ministers could get congregations in London,—it is a pity they have them anywhere,—men who cannot call a spade a spade, or a loaf of bread a loaf of bread. They are so refined, and speak such fine and polished language, that you would think they were not natives of England, and had never heard the people speak their own homely brogue. The Lord raise up among us men that speak market language, that have sympathy with the people, and that speak the people's tongue, and we shall prove that it is an infamous falsehood, that the causes cannot be maintained in poor neighbourhoods. They can be, and they *shall* be. Why, brethren, are we to say that we will give up the poor merely to the missionary ? We complain that the artizan will not come to hear ; that the fustian jacket will not listen. It is not true ; the fustian jacket is as ready to listen as is the broadcloth, if he had something to listen to. If it be the gospel, they that walk are as ready to come as they that ride, if they could but understand. I think that those who are gifted with this world's goods, or with this world's wisdom, will do right well, if instead of looking out for respectable positions, they will look out for the poorest positions, for there they will find the most of those whom God has chosen—the poor in this world, rich in faith, heirs of the kingdom. I would not say a word to set class against class ; for I suppose that the soul of a rich man is not less worth than the soul of the poorest ; all stand alike in the sight of God. But I do enter my solemn protest against men who say that the religion of Christ is not fit for the poor neighbourhoods, and only meant for our respectable suburbs. It is not true, brethren ; it is a great and gross heresy against the goodness of God, and against the adaptation of the gospel of Christ to the needs of the poor. They can sustain Churches. Look at the ragged churches in Glasgow and Edinburgh. They call them ragged ; but you see as clean faces and as intellectual countenances there as you would anywhere. If they find a man who can preach that they can hear, they will maintain and support him. The gospel of Christ will find as ready and faithful adherents among the poorest of the poor, as amongst the richest of the rich, and far more so in proportion.

Another homily, which you will think rather strange, is this—How wrong the Church of Christ is when it neglects the rich, "Well," you say, "that is not in the text ; it says these things were hidden from the wise and prudent." Yes, I know they were, but Christ thanked God they were. "I thank thee," he said "that thou hast hid these things." What then ? If I preach to the rich, to the wise, to the prudent, and they reject it, have I lost my toil ? No, no ; there is cause for thankfulness even then. We are to preach the gospel to every creature without any distinction whatever, high or low, great or small. "Well, but the wise and prudent will not hear it." We know that. But if they reject it still, there is matter for thankfulness that they heard it. "Why?" say you. Why because we are unto God a sweet smelling savour both in them that are saved and in them that perish. To the one we are a savour of life unto life, and to the other a savour of death unto death ; but to God still a sweet smelling savour. What! is God glorified in the damnation of the wise and prudent? Yes, tremendous fact! At the winding up of this world's drama, God will be glorified in the men that shut their eyes against his grace, as well as in the men whose eyes are opened to receive it. The yells of hell shall be but the deep bass of the everlasting music of which the songs in heaven are the *air*. God, the terrible one, shall have praise from the wise and prudent when their folly shall be discovered, when their wisdom shall be dashed in pieces or torn to shreds. God, the terrible avenger of his own gospel, shall be glorified when those are cast out, who having heard the gospel were too wise to believe it, and having listened to it were too prudent to give their praise to it. In either case God is glorified, and in either case Christ gives thanks, and devoutly gives thanks. To the rich, then, as well as to the poor ; to the hopeless case as well as to the hopeful ; to the wise as well as to the babe we should preach Christ, because even if they be not saved, yet still God is glorified. He getteth honour even upon Pharoah his enemy, when he perished in the midst of the sea.

And now, last of all, you who are babes, you who perhaps "know, and know no more than the Bible true," you who never read a word of Greek or Latin, and sometimes cannot spell the hard words of English, you say, "I do not go to a place of worship, I am so ignorant." Do you not perceive your own wickedness in stopping away? God hath revealed these things unto babes, and if there are any men that ought to come, certainly it is you. When the poor man says, "Oh, a place of worship is not for me," he is without excuse ; because the Scripture expressly says, "God has chosen the base things, and the things that are not, to bring to nought the things that are." I invite any man and every man to listen to the gospel, and if you do not come, you certainly do despite to every precious promise. You think the gospel is not meant for hard-working men, but it is just meant for you—for you above all others. You say, "Christ is a gentleman's Christ." No, he is the people's Christ. "I have exalted one chosen out of the people." Do you think our religion is meant for the learned? Not so ; it is meant for the most foolish and most ignorant. We rejoice to know that the poor have the gospel preached to them. But if they will not come and hear it, their guilt shall be sevenfold, seeing there were special words of comfort for them, there were choice sentences of invitation for them. If they do not come and listen, they must perish miserably, without the pretence of a shadow of a dream of an excuse. Ah, ye who are so poor that you scarce know where to lay your heads ; ye that are so ignorant that a ragged school might perhaps be your best academy, "Come ye, come buy wine and milk, without money and without price." Come ye as ye are to the great teacher of your souls. Trust him as you are ; trust his precious blood ; his glorious cross ; his intercession before the Eternal throne ; and you shall have reason to say in the words of the Master, "Father, I thank thee that thou hast hid these things from the wise and prudent, and hast revealed them unto babes. Even so, Father, for so it seemed good in thy sight."

The Two Effects
of the Gospel

"For we are unto God a sweet savour of Christ, in them that are saved, and in them that perish; to the one we are the savour of death unto death; and to the other the savour of life unto life. And who is sufficient for these things?"—2 Corinthians ii 15, 16.

THESE are the words of Paul, speaking on the behalf of himself and his brethren the Apostles, and they are true concerning all those who by the Spirit are chosen, qualified, and thrust into the vineyard to preach God's gospel. I have often admired the 14th verse of this chapter, especially when I have remembered from whose lips the words fell, " Now thanks be unto God, which always causeth us to triumph in Christ, and maketh manifest the savour of his knowledge by us in every place." Picture Paul, the aged, the man who had been beaten five times with "forty stripes save one," who had been dragged forth for dead, the man of great sufferings, who had passed through whole seas of persecution—only think of him saying, at the close of his ministerial career, " Now thanks be unto God, which always causeth us to triumph in Christ !" to triumph when shiprecked, to triumph when scourged, to triumph in the stocks, to triumph under the stones, to triumph amidst the hiss of the world, to triumph when he was driven from the city and shook off the dust from his feet, to triumph at all times in Christ Jesus! Now, if some ministers of modern times should talk thus, we would think little of it, for they enjoy the world's applause They can always go to their place in ease and peace; they have an admiring people, and no open foes; against them not a dog doth move his tongue; everything is safe and pleasant. For them to say, " Now thanks be unto God, which always causeth us to triumph " is a very little thing; but for one like Paul, so trampled on, so tried, so distressed, to say it—then, we say, outspoke a hero; here is a man who had true faith in God and in the divinity of his mission.

And, my brethren, how sweet is that consolation which Paul applied to his own heart amid all his troubles. "Notwithstanding all," he says, "God makes known the savour of his knowledge by us in every place." Ah! with this thought a minister may lay his head upon his pillow: "God makes manifest the savour of his knowledge." With this he may shut his eyes when his career is over, and with this he may open them in heaven: "God hath made known by me the savour of his knowledge in every place." Then follow the words of my text, of which I shall speak, dividing it into three particulars. Our first remark shall be, that *although the gospel is " a sweet savour" in every place, yet it produces different effects in different persons ;* " to one it is the savour of death unto death; and to the other the savour of life unto life." Our second observation shall be, that *ministers of the gospel are not responsible for their success,* for it is said, " We are unto God a sweet savour of Christ, in them that are saved, and in them that perish." And thirdly, *yet the gospel minister's place*

15

is by no means a light one : his duty is very weighty ; for the Apostle himself said, " Who is sufficient for these things?"

I. Our first remark is, that THE GOSPEL PRODUCES DIFFERENT EFFECTS. It must seem a strange thing, but it is strangely true, that there is scarcely ever a good thing in the world of which some little evil is not the consequence. Let the sun shine in brilliance—it shall moisten the wax, it shall harden clay; let it pour down floods of light on the tropics—it will cause vegetation to be extremely luxuriant, the richest and choicest fruits shall ripen, and the fairest of all flowers shall bloom, but who does not know, that there the worst of reptiles and the most venomous snakes are also brought forth? So it is with the gospel. Although it is the very sun of righteousness to the world, although it is God's best gift, although nothing can be in the least comparable to the vast amount of benefit which it bestows upon the human race, yet even of that we must confess, that sometimes it is the " savour of death unto death." But then we are not to blame the gospel for this; it is not the fault of God's truth; it is the fault of those who do not receive it. It is the " savour of life unto life" to every one that listens to its sound with a heart that is open to its reception. It is only " death unto death " to the man who hates the truth, despises it, scoffs at it, and tries to oppose its progress. It is of that character we must speak first.

1. The gospel is to *some* men " a savour of death unto death." Now, this depends very much upon what the gospel is; because there are some things called gospel, that are "a savour of death unto death" to everybody that hears them. John Berridge says he preached morality till there was not a moral man left in the village; and there is no way of injuring morality like legal preaching. The preaching of good works, and the exhorting men to holiness, as the means of salvation, is very much admired in theory; but when brought into practice, it is found not only in-effectual, but more than that—it becomes even " a savour of death unto death." So it has been found; and I think even the great Chalmers himself confessed, that for years and years before he knew the Lord, he preached nothing but morality and precepts, but he never found a drunkard reclaimed by shewing him merely the evils of drunkenness; nor did he find a swearer stop his swearing because he told him the heinousness of the sin; it was not until he began to preach the love of Jesus, in his great heart of mercy—it was not until he preached the gospel as it was in Christ, in some of its clearness, fulness, and power, and the doctrine, that " by grace ye are saved, through faith, and that not of yourselves, it is the gift of God" that he ever met with success. But when he did preach salvation by faith, by shoals the drunk-ards came from their cups, and swearers refrained their lips from evil speaking; thieves became honest men, and unrighteous and ungodly persons bowed to the sceptre of Jesus. But ye must confess, as I said before, that though the gospel does in the main produce the best effect upon almost all who hear it either by restraining them from sin, or constraining them to Christ, yet it is a great fact, and a solemn one, upon which I hardly know how to speak this morning, that to some men the preach-ing of Christ's gospel is " death unto death," and produces evil instead of good.

(1.) And the first sense is this. *Many men are hardened in their sins by hearing the gospel.* Oh! 'tis terribly and solemnly true, that of all sinners some sanctuary sin-ners are the worst. Those who can dive deepest into sin, and have the most quiet consciences and hardest hearts, are some who are to be found in God's own house. I know that a faithful ministry will often prick them, and the stern denunciations of a Boanerges will frequently make them shake. I am aware that the Word of God will sometimes make their blood curdle within them; but I know (for I have seen the men) that there are many who turn the grace of God into licentiousness, make even God's truth a stalking-horse for the devil, and abuse God's grace to palliate their sin. Such men have I found amongst those who hear the doctrines of grace in their fulness. They will say, "I am elect, therefore I may swear; I am one of those who were chosen of God before the foundation of the world, and therefore I may live as I list." I have seen the man who stood upon the table of a public house, and grasping the glass in his hand, said, "Mates! I can say more than any of you; I am one of those who arec edeemed with Jesus' precious blood:" and then he drank his tumbler of ale and danced again before them, and sang vile and blasphemous songs. Now, that is a man to whom the gospel is "a savour of death unto death." He hears the truth, but he perverts it; he takes what is intended by God for his good, and what does he do, he commits suicide therewith. That knife which was given him to open the secrets of the gospel he drives into his own heart. That which is the purest of all truth and the highest of all morality, he turns into the panderer of his vice, and makes it a scaffold to aid in building up his wickedness and sin. Are there any of you here like that man—who love to hear *the gospel*, as ye call it, and yet live impurely? who can sit down and say you are the children of God, and still behave like liege servants of the devil? Be it known unto you, that ye are liars and hypocrites, for the truth is not in you at all. "If any man is born of God, he cannot sin." God's elect will not be suffered to fall into continual sin; they will never "turn the grace of God into licentiousness;" but it will be their endeavour, as much as in them lies, to keep near to Jesus. Rest assured of this: "By their fruits ye shall know them." "A good tree cannot bring forth corrupt fruit; neither can an evil tree bring forth good fruit." Such men, however, are continually turning the gospel into evil. They sin with a high hand, from the very fact that they have heard what they consider excuses their vice. There is nothing under heaven, I conceive, more liable to lead men astray than a perverted gospel. A truth perverted is generally worse than a doctrine which all know to be false. As fire, one of the most useful of the elements, can also cause the fiercest of conflagrations, so the gospel, the best thing we have, can be turned to the vilest account. This is one sense in which it is "a savour of death unto death."

(2). But another. It is a fact that *the gospel of Jesus Christ will increase some men's damnation at the last great day.* Again, I startle at myself when I have said it; for it seems too horrible a thought for us to venture to utter—that the gospel of Christ will make hell hotter to some men than it otherwise would have been. Men would all have sunk to hell had it not been for the gospel. The grace of God reclaims "a multitude that no man can number;" it secures a countless army who shall be saved in the Lord with an everlasting salvation;" but, at the same time, it does to those who reject it, make their damnation even more dreadful. And let me tell you why.

First, *because men sin against greater light;* and the light we have is an excellent measure of our guilt. What a Hottentot might do without a crime, would be the greatest sin to me, because I am taught better; and what some even in London might do with impunity—set down, as it might be, as a sin by God, but not so exceeding sinful—would be to me the very height of transgression, because I have from my youth up been tutored to piety. The gospel comes upon men like the light from heaven. What a wanderer must he be who strays in the light! If he who is blind falls into the ditch we can pity him, but if a man, with the light on his eyeballs dashes himself from the precipice and loses his own soul, is not pity out of the question?

> "How they *deserve* the deepest hell,
> That slight the joys above!
> What chains of vengeance must they feel,
> Who laugh at sov'reign love!"

It will increase your condemnation, I tell you all, unless you find Jesus Christ to be your Saviour; for to have had the light and not to walk by it, shall be *the* condemnation, the very essence of it. This shall be the virus of the guilt—that the "light came into the world, and the darkness comprehended it not;" for "men love darkness rather than light, because their deeds are evil."

Again: it must increase your condemnation if you *oppose the gospel*. If God devises a scheme of mercy, and man rises up against it, how great must be his sin? Who shall tell the great guilt incurred by such men as Pilate, Herod, and the Jews? Oh! who shall picture out, or even faintly sketch, the doom of those who cried, "Crucify him! Crucify him!" And who shall tell what place in hell shall be hot enough for the man who slanders God's minister, who speaks against his people, who hates his truth, who would, if he could, utterly cut off the godly from the land? Ah! God help the infidel! God help the blasphemer! God save his soul: for of all men least would I choose to be that man. Think you, sirs, that God will not take account of what men have said? One man has cursed Christ; he has called him a charlatan. Another has declared, (knowing that he spoke a lie) that the gospel was false. A third has proclaimed his licentious maxims, and then has pointed to God's Word, and said, "There are worse things there!" A fourth has abused God's ministers and held up their imperfections to ridicule. Think you God shall forget all this at the last day? When his enemies come before him, shall he take them by the hand and say, "The other day thou didst call my servant a dog, and spit on him, and for this I will give thee heaven!" Rather, if the sin has not been cancelled by the blood of Christ, will he not say, "Depart, cursed one, into the hell which thou didst scoff at; leave that heaven which thou didst despise; and learn that though thou saidst there was no God, this right arm shall teach thee eternally the lesson that there is one; for he who discovers it not by my works of benevolence shall learn it by my deeds of vengeance: therefore depart, again, I say!" It *shall* increase men's hell that they have opposed God's truth. Now, is not this a very solemn view of the gospel, that it is indeed to many "a savour of death unto death?"

(3). Yet, once more: I believe *the gospel makes some men in this world more miserable than they would be.* The drunkard could drink, and could revel in his intoxication with greater joy, if he did not hear it said, "All drunkards shall have their portion in the lake that burneth with fire and brimstone." How jovially the Sabbath-breaker would riot through his Sabbaths, if the Bible did not say, "Remember the Sabbath day to keep it holy!" And how happily could the libertine and licentious man drive on his mad career, if he were not told, "The wages of sin is death, and after death the judgment!" But the truth puts the bitter in his cup; the warnings of God freeze the current of his soul. The gospel is like the skeleton at the Egyptian feast. Though by day he laughed at it, by night he will quiver as the aspen leaf, and when the shades of evening gather around him, he will shake at a whisper. At the thought of a future state his joy is spoiled, and immortality, instead of being a boon to him, is in its very contemplation the misery of his existence. The sweet wooings of mercy are to him no more harmonious than peals of thunder, because he knows he despises them. Yea, I have known some who have been in such misery under the gospel, because they would not give up their sins, that they have been ready to take their own lives. Oh! terrible thought! The gospel is "a savour of death unto death!" Unto how many here is it so? Who are now hearing God's Word to be damned by it? Who shall retire hence to be hardened by the sound of the truth? Why, every man who does not believe it; for unto those that receive it, it is "a savour of life unto life," but to unbelievers it is a curse, and "a savour of death unto death."

2. But, blessed be God, the gospel has a second power. Besides being "death unto death," it is "a savour of life unto life." Ah! my brethren, some of us could speak, if we were allowed this morning, of the gospel as being "a savour of life" to us. We can look back to that hour when we were "dead in trespasses and sins." In vain all Sinai's thunders; in vain the rousing of the watchmen; we slept on in the death-sleep of our transgressions; nor could an angel have aroused us. But we look back with joy to that hour when first we stepped within the walls of a sanctuary, and savingly heard the voice of mercy. With some of you it is but a few weeks· I know where ye are and who ye are. But a few weeks or months ago ye too were far from God, but now ye are brought to love him. Canst thou look back

my brother Christian, to that very moment when the gospel was "a savour of life" to thee—when thou didst cast away thy sins, renounce thy lusts, and turning to God's Word, received it with full purpose of heart? Ah! that hour—of all hours the sweetest! Nothing can be compared therewith. I knew a person who for forty or fifty years had been completely deaf. Sitting one morning at her cottage door as some vehicle was passing, she thought she heard melodious music. It was not music; it was but the sound of the vehicle. Her ear had suddenly opened, and that rough sound seemed to her like the music of heaven, because it was the first she had heard for so many years. Even so, the first time our ears were opened to hear the words of love—the assurance of our pardon—we never heard the word so well as we did then; it never seemed so sweet; and perhaps, even now, we look back and say,

> "What peaceful hours I then enjoyed!
> How sweet their memory still!"

When first it was "a savour of life" unto our souls.

Then, beloved, if it ever has been "a savour of life," it will *always* be "a savour of life;" because it says it is not a savour of life unto death, but "a savour of life unto life." Now I must aim another blow at my antagonists the Arminians; I cannot help it. They will have it that sometimes the gospel is a savour of life unto death. They tell us that a man may receive spiritual life, and yet may die eternally. That is to say, a man may be forgiven, and yet be punished afterwards; he may be justified from all sin, and yet after that, his transgressions can be laid on his shoulders again. A man may be born of God, and yet die; a man may be loved of God, and yet God may hate him to-morrow. Oh! I cannot bear to speak of such doctrines of lies; let those believe them that like. As for me, I so deeply believe in the immutable love of Jesus that I suppose that if one believer were to be in hell, Christ himself would not long stay in heaven, but would soon cry, "To the rescue! to the rescue!" Oh! if Jesus Christ were in glory with one of the gems wanting in his crown, and Satan had that gem in hell, he would say, "Aha! prince of light and glory, I have one of thy jewels!" and he would hold it up, and then he would say, "Aha! thou didst die for this man, but thou hadst not strength enough to save him; thou didst love him once—where is thy love? It is not worth having, for thou didst hate him afterwards!" And how would he chuckle over that heir of heaven, and hold him up, and say, "This man was redeemed; Jesus Christ purchased him with his blood:" and plunging him in the waves of hell, he would say, "There purchased one! see how I can rob the Son of God!" And then again he would say, "This man was forgiven; behold the justice of a God! He is to be punished after he is forgiven. Christ suffered for this man's sins, and yet," says Satan with a malignant joy, "I have him afterwards; for God exacted the punishment twice!" Shall that e'er be said? Ah! no. It is "a savour of life unto life," and not of life unto death. Go, with your vile gospel; preach it where you please; but my Master said, "I give unto my sheep eternal life." You give to your sheep temporary life, and they lose it; but, says Jesus, "I give unto my sheep ETERNAL life, and they shall never perish, neither shall any man pluck them out of my hands." I generally wax warm when I get to this subject, because I think few doctrines more vital than that of the perseverance of the saints; for if ever one child of God did perish, or if I knew it were possible that one could, I should conclude at once that I must, and I suppose each of you would do the same; and then where is the joy and happiness of the gospel? Again I tell you the Arminian gospel is the shell without the kernel; it is the husk without the fruit; and those who love it may take it to themselves. We will not quarrel with them. Let them go and preach it. Let them go and tell poor sinners, that if they believe in Jesus they will be damned after all, that Jesus Christ will forgive them, and yet the Father send them to hell. Go and preach your gospel, and who will listen to it? And if they do listen, is it worth their hearing? I say no; for if I am to stand after conversion on the same footing as I did before conversion, then it is of no use for me to have been converted at all. But whom he loves he loves to the end.

> "Once in Christ, in Christ for ever;
> Nothing from his love can sever."

It is "a savour of life unto life." And not only "life unto life" in this world, but "of life unto life" eternal. Every one who has this life shall receive the next life; for "the Lord will give grace and glory, and no good thing will he withhold from them that walk uprightly."

I am obliged to leave this point; but if my Master will but take it up, and make his word "a savour of life unto life" this morning, I shall rejoice in what I have said.

II. But our second remark was, that THE MINISTER IS NOT RESPONSIBLE FOR HIS SUCCESS. He *is* responsible for what he preaches; he is accountable for his life and actions; but he is not responsible for other people. If I do but preach God's word, if there never were a soul saved, the King would say, "Well done, good and faithful servant!" If I do but tell my message, if none should listen to it, he would say, "Thou hast fought the good fight: receive thy crown." You hear the words of the text: "We are unto God a sweet savour of Christ, as well in them that perish, as in them that are saved." This will appear, if I just tell you what a gospel minister is called in the Bible. Sometimes he is called an *ambassador*. Now, for what is an ambassador responsible? He goes to a country as a plenipotentiary; he carries terms of peace to the conference; he uses all his talents for his master; he tries to show that the war is inimical to the prosperity of the different countries; he endeavours to bring about peace; but the other kings haughtily refuse it. When he comes home does his master say, "Why did not you make peace?" "Why, my Lord," he would say, "I told them the terms; but they said nothing." "Well, then," he will say, "thou hast done thy duty; I am not to condemn thee if the war continues." Again: the minister of the gospel is called a *fisherman*. Now a fisherman is not responsible for the quantity of fish he catches, but for the way he fishes. That is a mercy for some ministers, I am sure, for they have neither caught fish, nor even attracted any round their nets. They have been spending all their life fishing with most elegant silk lines, and gold and silver hooks; they always use nicely polished phrases; but the fish will not bite for all that, whereas we of a rougher order have put the hook into the jaws of hundreds. However, if we cast the gospel net in the right place, even if we catch none, the Master will find no fault with us. He will say, "Fisherman! didst thou labour? Didst thou throw the net into the sea in the time of storms?" "Yes, my Lord, I did." "What hast thou caught?" "Only one or two." "Well, I could have sent thee a shoal, if it so pleased me; it is not thy fault; I give in my sovereignty where I please; or withhold when I choose; but as for thee, thou hast well laboured, therefore there is thy reward." Sometimes the minister is called a *sower*. Now, no farmer expects a sower to be responsible for the harvest; all he is responsible for is, does he sow the seed? and does he sow the right seed? If he scatters it on good soil, then he is happy; but if it falls by the way-side, and the fowls of the air devour it, who shall blame the sower? Could he help it? Nay, he did his duty; he scattered the seed broad-cast, and there he left it. Who is to blame? Certainly not the sower. So, beloved, if a minister comes to heaven with but one sheaf on his shoulder, his Master will say, "O reaper! once a sower! where didst thou gather thy sheaf?" "My Lord, I sowed upon the rock, and it would not grow; only one seed on a chance Sabbath-morning was blown a little awry by the wind, and it fell on a prepared heart; and this is my one sheaf." "Hallelujah!" the angelic choirs resound, "one sheaf from a rock is more honour to God than a thousand sheaves from a good soil; therefore, let him take his seat as near the throne as yon man, who, stooping beneath his many sheaves, comes from some fertile land, bringing his sheaves with him." I believe that if there are degrees in glory, they will not be in proportion to success, but in proportion to the earnestness of our endeavours. If we mean right, and if with all our heart we strive to do the right thing as ministers if we never see any effect, still shall we receive the crown. But how much more happy is the man who shall have it in heaven said to him, "He shines for ever, because he was wise, and won many souls unto righteousness." It is always my greatest joy to believe, that if I should enter heaven, I shall in future days see heaven's gates open, and in shall fly a cherub, who, looking me in the face, will smilingly pass along to God's throne, and there bow down before him; and when he has paid his homage and his adoration, he may fly to me, and though unknown, shall clasp my hand, and if there were tears in heaven, surely I should weep, and he would say, "Brother, from thy lips I heard the word;

thy voice first admonished me of my sin; here I am, and thou the instrument of my salvation." And as the gates open one after another, still will they come in; souls ransomed, souls ransomed; and for each one of these a star—for each one of these another gem in the diadem of glory—for each one of them another honour, and another note in the song of praise. Blessed be that man that shall die in the Lord, and his works shall follow him; for thus saith the Spirit.

What will become of some good Christians now in Exeter Hall, if crowns in heaven are measured in value by the souls that are saved? Some of you will have a crown in heaven without a single star in it. I read a little while ago, a piece upon the starless crown in heaven—a man in heaven with a crown without a star! Not one saved by him! He will sit in heaven as happy as he can be, for sovereign mercy saved him; but oh! to be in heaven without a single star! Mother! what sayest thou to be in heaven without one of thy children to deck thy brow with a star? Minister! what wouldst thou say to be a polished preacher, and yet have no star? Writer! will it well become thee to have written even as gloriously as Milton, if thou shouldst be found in heaven without a star? I am afraid we pay too little regard to this. Men will sit down and write huge folios and tomes, that they may have them put in libraries for ever, and have their names handed down by fame! but how few are looking to win stars for ever in heaven! Toil on, child of God, toil on; for if thou wishest to serve God, thy bread cast upon the waters shall be found after many days. If thou sendest in the feet of the ox or the ass, thou shalt reap a glorious harvest in that day when he comes to gather in his elect. The minister is not responsible for his success.

III. But yet, in the last place, TO PREACH THE GOSPEL IS HIGH AND SOLEMN WORK. The ministry has been very often degraded into a trade. In these days men are taken and made into ministers who would have made good captains at sea, who could have waited well at the counter, but who were never intended for the pulpit. They are selected by man; they are crammed with literature; they are educated up to a certain point; they are turned out ready dressed; and persons call them ministers. I wish them all God-speed, every one of them; for as good Joseph Irons used to say, "God be with many of them, if it be only to make them hold their tongues." Man-made ministers are of no use in this world, and the sooner we get rid of them the better. Their way is this: they prepare their manuscripts very carefully, then read it on the Sunday most sweetly in *sotto voce*, and so the people go away pleased. But that is not God's way of preaching. If so, I am sufficient to preach for ever. I can buy manuscript sermons for a shilling; that is to say, provided they have been preached fifty times before, but if I use them for the first time the price is a guinea, or more. But that is not the way. Preaching God's word is not what some seem to think, mere child's play—a mere business or trade to be taken up by any one. A man ought to feel first that he has a solemn call to it; next, he ought to know that he really possesses the Spirit of God, and that when he speaks there is an influence upon him that enables him to speak as God would have him, otherwise out of the pulpit he should go directly; he has no right to be there, even if the living is his own property. He has not been called to preach God's truth, and unto him God says, "What hast thou to do, to declare my statutes?"

But you say, "What is there difficult about preaching God's gospel?" Well it must be somewhat hard; for Paul said, "Who is sufficient for these things?" And first I will tell you, it is difficult because it is so hard as not to be warped by your own prejudices in preaching the word. You want to say a stern thing; and your heart says, "Master! in so doing thou wilt condemn thyself;" then the temptation is not to say it. Another trial is, you are afraid of displeasing the rich in your congregations. Your think, "If I say such-and-such a thing, so-and-so will be offended; such an one does not approve of that doctrine; I had better leave it out." Or perhaps you will happen to win the applause of the multitude, and you must not say anything that will displease them, for if they cry, "Hosanna" to day, they will cry, "Crucify, crucify," to-morrow. All these things work on a minister's heart. He is a man like yourselves; and he feels it. Then comes again the sharp knife of criticism, and the arrows of those who hate him and hate his Lord; and he cannot help feeling it sometimes. He may put on his armour, and cry, "I care not for your malice;" but there were seasons when the archers sorely grieved even Joseph. Then he stands in another danger, lest he should come out and defend himself; for he is a great fool whoever tries to do it. He who lets his detractors alone, and like the eagle cares not for the chattering of the sparrows, or like the lion will not turn aside to rend the snarling jackal—he is the man, and he shall be honoured. But the danger is, we want to set ourselves right. And oh! who is sufficient to steer clear from these rocks of danger? "Who is sufficient," my brethren, "for these things?"—To stand up, and to proclaim, Sabbath after Sabbath, and week-day after week day, "the unsearchable riches of Christ."

Having said thus much, I may draw the inference—to close up—which is: if the gospel is "a savour of life unto life," and if the minister's work be solemn work, how well it becomes all lovers of the truth to plead for all those who preach it, that they may be "sufficient for these things." To lose my Prayer-book, as I have often told you, is the worst thing that can happen to me. To have no one to pray for me would place me in a dreadful condition. "Perhaps," says a good poet, "the day when the world shall perish, will be the day unwhitened by a prayer;" and, perhaps, the day when a minister turned aside from truth, was the day when his people left off to pray for him, and when there was not a single voice supplicating grace on his behalf. I am sure it must be so with me. Give me the numerous hosts of men whom it has been my pride and glory to see in my place before I came to this hall: give me those praying people, who on the Monday evening met in such a multitude to pray to God for a blessing, and we will overcome hell itself, in spite of all that may oppose us. All our perils are nothing, so long as we have prayer. But increase my congregation; give me the polite and the noble,—give me influence and understanding,—and I should fail to do anything without a praying church. My people! shall I ever lose your prayers? Will ye ever cease your supplications? Our toils are nearly ended in this great place, and happy shall we be to return to our much-loved sanctuary. Will ye then ever cease to pray? I fear ye have not uttered so many prayers this morning as ye should have done; I fear there has not been so much earnest devotion as might have been poured forth. For my own part, I have not felt the wondrous power I sometimes experience. I will not lay it at your doors; but never let it be said, "Those people, once so fervent, have become cold!" Let not Laodiceanism get into Southwark; let us leave it here in the West-end, if it is to be anywhere; let us not carry it with us. Let us "strive together for the faith once delivered unto the saints:" and knowing in what a sad position the standard-bearer stands, I beseech you rally round him; for it will be ill with the army,

> "If the standard-bearer fall, as fall full well he may.
> For never saw I promise yet, of such a deadly fray."

Stand up my friends; grasp the banner yourselves, and maintain it erect until the day shall come, when standing on the last conquered castle of hell's domains, we shall raise the shout, "Hallelujah! Hallelujah! Hallelujah! The Lord God Omnipotent reigneth!" Till that time, fight on.

Christ Manifesting Himself to His People

"Judas saith unto him, not Iscariot, Lord, how is it that thou wilt manifest thyself unto us, and not unto the world?"—John xiv. 22.

WHAT a blessed Master Jesus Christ was! How familiar did he allow his disciples to make themselves with him! Though he was the Lord of life and glory, the great and mighty one, as well as the man of Nazareth, yet see how he talks with his poor disciples, the fishermen, just as if he had been one of the same class and order with themselves! He was none of your dignitaries who pride themselves on that dignity—none of those ecclesiastics who love to carry much of formality about them, and to walk above other men, as if they were not indeed their fellows; but he talks to his disciples just as a father would to his children—even more kindly than a master might to his pupils. He lets them put the simplest questions to him, and instead of rebuking them for their familiarity, he condescends to answer everything they please to ask him. Philip uttered a sentence which one would think no sensible man, who had been so long time with Jesus, ever could have troubled him with. He said, "Show us the Father and it sufficeth us." A stupid idea! As if Jesus Christ could shew the Father; that is to say, could shew God to Philip! And Jesus kindly answered—"Hast thou been so long time with me, and yet hast thou not known me, Philip? Believest thou not that I am in the Father, and the Father in me? He that hath seen me hath seen the Father." And now comes Judas (not Iscariot); and he puts also a very simple and easy question—one he needed not to have asked; but Jesus Christ, instead of rebuking him, simply passes on to another subject, and forbears most wisely to answer the enquiry, because he would teach him more by silence than he could do by an explanation.

We must also notice here how very particular the Holy Ghost is that a good man should not be confounded with a bad one. He says, "Judas, not Iscariot." There were two of the name of Judas; the one who betrayed our Lord, and the other who wrote the epistle of Jude, who should properly have been called Judas. Some of us, in reading the name Judas, might have said, "Ah! it was that traitor Judas Iscariot that asked the question." But the Holy Spirit would not allow this mistake to be made. This again should teach us, that it is not an idle wish for us to desire that our name should be handed down to posterity. We ought all to wish to have an unblemished character; we ought to desire to have that promise fulfilled, "The memory of the just is blessed." I would not wish my name to be mistaken for that of some criminal who was hanged. I would not wish to have my name written even by mistake in the calendar of infamy. However much I may now be misrepresented, it will one day be known that I have honestly striven for the glory of my Master; and God will say, "Judas, not Iscariot." The man was no deceiver after all.

But we will now forsake Judas altogether, and proceed to look at our text. It contains two things: first, *an important fact*; secondly, *an interesting enquiry*. "Lord, how is it that thou wilt manifest thyself unto us, and not unto the world?" Here is a fact, and an enquiry concerning it.

I. First, then, here is A GREAT FACT: that Jesus Christ does reveal himself to his people, but he does not unto the world. The fact is implied in the question; and even if Scripture did not declare it to be the truth, there are many of us who have a Scripture written in our hearts—the Bible of experience—which teaches us that it is true. Ask Christian men whether they have not had manifestations of their Lord and Saviour Jesus Christ, in a peculiar and wonderful manner, such as they never felt when they were in their unregenerate state. Turn to the biographies of eminent saints, and you will find there instances recorded in which Jesus has been pleased, in a very special manner to speak to their souls, to unfold the wonders of his person, and let them discern the matchless glories of his office; yea, so have their souls been steeped in happiness that they have thought themselves to be in heaven, whereas they were not there though they were well nigh on the threshold of it—for when Jesus manifests himself to his people, it is a young heaven on earth, it is a paradise in embryo, it is the beginning of the bliss of the glorified; yea, and it shall be the consummation of that bliss, when Jesus Christ shall perfectly unveil himself to the admiring eyes of all his people and they shall be like him, and shall see him as he his.

We are about to talk somewhat this morning, then, concerning that special manifestation which Jesus Christ vouchsafes to his people, and to his people only. We will make four observations here. We will observe, first, something concerning the favoured persons—"unto *us*," "not unto the world." Secondly, concerning special seasons—"How is it that thou *wilt*?" He was not doing it just then; but "thou wilt." There are special seasons. Thirdly, some remarks concerning the wonderful display—"Thou wilt manifest *thyself* unto us, as thou dost not unto the world." Then, fourthly, we shall dwell a little upon *the effects* which this manifestation will produce upon our souls.

1. First, then, who are the favored people to whom Jesus Christ manifests himself? "How is it that thou wilt manifest thyself unto *us*, and not unto the world?" It appears from the text that the persons to whom Jesus Christ shews himself in this wonderful manner do not belong to the world. Who, then, are these people? I am sure it would be difficult for you or me to discover them; I shall, therefore, this morning employ a fiction, and shall bid some spirit from an unknown world point out these distinguished individuals. O spirit! I give thee an errand. There are a certain number of people *in* this world who are not *of* it: go thou, search them out, and come thou back and tell me what thou hast found. We give the spirit time; he flies round the world, and he returns. "I have seen," says he, "a multitude of men; they are all pursuing one common path, with one object; I have seen them trampling on each other in the fury of their hot pursuit; I have seen them hurrying after something which each one desired for himself; but in the midst of the throng I saw a few marching in an opposite direction, who with much elbowing and strong opposition were going exactly contrary to the stream. I saw written on the foreheads of those who were proceeding with the crowd, the word 'Self;' but I marked those who were proceeding in the other direction, and behold, they had inscribed upon their brows, 'Christ;' and as I listened to them frequently in their soliloquies, I heard them say, 'For us to live is Christ, for us to die is gain.' I marked these men, I saw them constantly pursuing their way in the teeth of all defiance, going against every opposition; I wondered where they were going; and I saw that before them was a wicket-gate, and on it the words; 'Mercy for the chief of sinners.' I saw them enter there; I marked them as they ran along the walls of salvation, and tracking them along to their destination, I saw them at

24

last fold their arms in death, shut their eyes with tranquility; while I heard angels sing their requiem, and a voice shouted, 'Blessed are the dead that die in the Lord.' Surely these must be the persons who are not of the world." Thou hast spoken rightly, O spirit; these are the individuals. What didst thou see of them, O spirit? Did they assemble and congregate together; or did they mix with the rest of humanity? "Why," saith he, "I noticed that once in the week they crowded to a certain place they called the House of God; I heard their song of praise; I saw them bend their knee in reverence, not only in that house, but in private; I witnessed their groanings, their strugglings, and their agonies; I knew that they were men of prayer, and men that loved God. I saw them gather in secret assemblies, to tell what the Lord had done for their souls; I marked that they would not be found with the wicked. I saw some houses that they would not enter. At the corner of the street there stood a house, well lighted up with many a lamp; and there were on its front some mystic cabalistic signs, the marks of woe and ill-doings. I saw the wicked there, reeling to and fro; I observed them in their drunkenness. But I marked how the Christian man put up his hand before his eyes, and passed by that place. I saw too another haunt of hell, where there were enacted scenes that eye should not have beheld—where shouts of revelry and mirth, but not songs of holiness, were heard. I looked round that theatre, and I discerned not a single one of these blessed persons; they would not run in the ways of the wicked, nor sit in the seat of the scorner, nor stand in the council of the unrighteous. I marked that like 'birds of a feather they would flock together'—that they found their mates, and there they went—that they built their nest in the same tree, and would make their habitation beneath the self-same roof." "Yea," saith the spirit, "I heard one of them exclaim, 'He that telleth lies shall not abide in my sight.' I saw him drive the liar from his house, and bid the profligate depart from him. I marked them; they were a select and separate people; and I said, surely these are the men of whom it is written, 'They shall dwell alone, they shall not be numbered among the people.'" Well, spirit, rightly hast thou described them. I wonder how many there are here; the men to whom God will reveal himself, and not to the world. They are men who are not worldly in principle, in action, in conversation, in desires, in object, or in end. These are the persons. Do not tell me anything about universal grace, or universal manifestations, while I have the power I will proclaim free grace to peculiar characters, as long as I find it written, "Thou wilt manifest thyself to us, but not to the world."

Our next remark is concerning *special seasons*. These highly favoured men do not always see Jesus Christ alike. They do not always live in the sunshine of his countenance. There are special times when God is pleased to reveal himself to his people. And these seasons are generally of two kinds: times of duty, and times of trial. I never found a lazy or indifferent Christian have a manifestation of Jesus Christ; I never heard one who gave himself wholly to business talk much of spiritual manifestations. No, poor soul; he had got religion enough to save him, but not enough to make him realize the spiritual and special blessings of a Christian. Those who do but little for Christ, Christ does but little for them in the way of special favors. Those who sit down, fold their arms, eat, drink, and are satisfied, are not the men who enter into the secret chamber of the Most High, and enjoy the presence of the Almighty. The men who are the most zealous for their Master discern the most of his loving-kindness, and enjoy the richest blessings from the Lord. Ask a Christian when he is the happiest, he will say, when he works the most. I know I am. I have not tried rest yet, and no doubt I shall find it anything but rest when I have it. When I pass a day without preaching my Master's name I feel that I have not done what I ought to have done, and I do not rest satisfied till I am within the four boards of a pulpit again. When we work the hardest we feel grace the most plentiful; when we dig the deepest we get the sweetest water. He who toils the most has his bread the most sweetened; and depend upon it, drops of sweat are blessed things to make dry bread go down. We shall always have more happiness the more we labor for Christ. As for Issachar, who is a strong ass, crouching down between two burdens—the man who is doing little— the pre...use is, "A whip for the horse, a bridle for the ass, and a rod for the fool's back." The man who is idle must have chastisement; but he who serves his Goa may rejoice, for God will treat him with dainties; he will give him his portion mixed with honey; he will say, "I have taken thy bread and dipped it in my own dish; take it, and eat it, for thou art one who works in my own vineyard." It will be in seasons of duty, or, as I have said, in seasons of trial; for you must not suppose when a Christian is laid aside from duty that he is doing nothing. Do not imagine that the time of your sickness has been lost to you. You were not only profiting yourselves, but actually serving God by your suffering, if you bore it patiently. Don't you know the text—"We fill up that which is behind of the sufferings of Christ, for his body's sake, which is the church." Christ's mystical body you are aware is made up of the head and all the members. The head had a certain amount to suffer—that is all finished; but the body has a measured portion to endure also; and the more *you* suffer so much the less suffering there is for somebody else. There is a certain quantum of trial which the whole church has to sustain before it gets to heaven; for as Jesus Christ was afflicted, even so the whole of his people must have fellowship with his sufferings. There is a cup that is full of mixture, and the righteous must drink it; we must all have a sip thereof; but if one of us can take a deep draught, and do it patiently, there is so much the less for our fellows. Let us not complain, then; for it is in the time of trouble we see most of Jesus. Before Israel fought Amalek, God gave them water from the rock, and sent them manna from heaven; and before Jacob met Esau, the angel of God wrestled with him at the brook Jabbok, and hosts of angels met him at Mahanaim. Previous to trial you may generally expect a season of joy; and when that season of joy is over, you may say, "We must expect some danger now, for we have received too much delight." But when the trial comes, then expect to have delight with it; for our troubles are generally proportioned to our joys, and our joys are usually proportioned to our troubles. The more bitter the vessel of grief, the sweeter the cup of consolation; the heavier weight of trial here, the brighter the crown of glory hereafter. In fact, the same word in Hebrew signifies "weight" and "glory." A weight of trouble is a glory to a Christian, for it is an honor to him; and glory is a weight, for it often bows him down, and makes him lie low at his Master's feet. I appeal to my brothers and sisters, and ask them when it is they have seen most of Jesus—when they have been walking in the garden of delights, or when the bitter medicine has been in their mouth. Have you not had better visions of Jesus, when you have been racked with pain, than when you have been elevated by prosperity? When the barn has been full, the oil vat has been bursting, and the wine has been running over, it is often then that the sanctuary of God has been forsaken and the cabinet of God's loving-kindness is nearly disregarded. But when the fig-tree does not blossom, and when there are no herds in the stalls, then it is that God often comes nearest to his children, and most reveals himself to them.

2. The next thought is, *the wondrous display itself.* Jesus Christ manifest *himself.* There are many manifestations of God to his children; but this is the most precious of all. Some manifestations we never wish to have again. We do not want to have that discovery which we had of our sinfulness, when first we were awakened: we will leave it to God, but we will never pray for it. But here is a manifestation we should like to have every day. "I will manifest myself to him." He does this in different ways. I have had for a long while a manifestation of his sufferings in Gethsemane; I have been for months musing on his agonies; I think I have even eaten the bitter herbs that grow there, and drank of that black brook Kedron. I have sometimes gone up stairs alone, to put myself in the very posture Jesus Christ was in; and I thought I could sympathize with him in his sufferings. Methought I saw the sweat of blood falling down to the ground; I had so sweet a view of my Saviour in his agonies. I hope that one day I may be able to accompany him still further, and see him on Calvary, and hear his death-shriek, "Eli, Eli, lama sabachthani?" Some of you, I know, have seen Jesus with the eye of faith quite as plainly as if

you had seen him with your natural eyes. You could see your Saviour hanging on the cross. You thought you saw the very crown of thorns on his head, and the drops of blood streaming down his face; you heard his cry; you saw his bleeding side; you beheld the nails, and before long you could have gone and pulled them out, and wrapped him up in linen and spices, and carried his body and washed it with tears and anointed it with precious ointment. At other times you have had a manifestation of Christ in his gifts. You have seen that mighty sacrifice he offered, the pile smoking up to heaven, and all your sins burnt up with it; you have seen clearly the justifying righteousness he has put upon you; and as you have looked at yourselves you have said—

> " Strangely, my soul, art thou arrayed.
> By the great sacred Three ;
> In sweetest harmony of praise,
> Let all my powers agree."

There are times when you have felt much joy at the exaltation of Jesus Christ, as displayed in his gifts. Then, again, you will see him in his triumph, with one foot upon Satan, and the other upon death. You will be able to behold him, marching up the sky, with all the glittering hosts behind him; and in due time you will have a manifestation of him to your soul, as sitting on his Father's throne until his enemies are made his footstool. And faith will sometimes so outsoar the wings of time, that we can bring futurity to the present, and see that great and pompous appearance, when on the great white throne the king shall sit and grasp his sceptre, and when his saints before him shall shout his praise. If I were to go much farther, I should be accused of fanaticism, and so it may be; but yet I will believe and must believe that there are seasons when the Christian lives next door to heaven. If I have not gone within an inch of the pearly gates I am not here; if I have not sometimes snuffed the incense from the censers of the glorified and heard the music of their harps, I think I am not a living man. There have been seasons of ecstatic joy, when I have climbed the highest mountains, and I have caught some sweet whisper from the throne. Have you had such manifestations? I will not condemn you if you have not : but I believe most Christians have them, and if they are much in duty and much in suffering they will have them. It is not given to all to have that portion, but to some it is, and such men know what religion means. I was reading a short time ago of a Mr. Tennant. He was about to preach one evening, and thought he would take a walk. As he was walking in a wood he felt so overpoweringly the presence of Christ, and such a manifestation of him, that he knelt down, and they could not discover him at the hour when he was to have preached. He continued there for hours, insensible as to whether he was in the body or out of the body; and when they waked him he looked like a man who had been with Jesus, and whose face shone. He never should forget, he said, to his dying day, that season of communion, when positively, though he could not see Christ, Christ was there, holding fellowship with him, heart against heart, in the sweetest manner. A wondrous display it must have been. You must know something of it, if not much ; otherwise you have not gone far on your spiritual course. God teach you more, and lead you deeper! " Then shall ye know, when ye follow on to know the Lord."

4. Then, *what will be the natural effects of this spiritual manifestation?* The first effect will be *humility.* If a man says, "I have had such and such spiritual communications, I am a great man;" he has never had any communications at all; for "God has respect unto the humble, but the proud he knoweth *afar off.*" He does not want to come near them to know them, and will never give them any visits of love. It will give a man *happiness;* for he must be happy who lives near to God. Again : it will give a man *holiness.* A man who has not holiness has never had this manifestation. Some men profess a great deal ; but do not believe any man unless you see that his deeds answer to what he says. "Be not deceived, God is not mocked." He will not bestow his favors upon the wicked ; for while he will not cast away a perfect man, neither will he respect an evil doer. Thus there will three effects of nearness to Jesus, all beginning with the letter *h*— humility, happiness, and holiness. May God give them to us!

II. Now for the second point : AN INTERESTING INQUIRY. Judas said, "How is it that thou wilt manifest thyself unto us, and not unto the world?" How was this inquiry suggested, and how was it answered.

First, it was suggested by *ignorance.* Poor Judas thought—"How can Jesus manifest himself to us, and not to the world? Why, if he comes down again, the world will see him as well as we do. How can he do it? Suppose he appears in a chariot of fire, or descends in a cloudy pillar : if we see him, the world must see him too." So, poor thing, he very ignorantly said, "How can it be, Lord?" Perhaps, too, the question was put by reason of his *great kindness.* "Ah! Lord," said he, "how can it be that thou wilt manifest thyself to us, and not unto the world?" He was slightly an Arminian ; he wanted it all to be given to everybody; and he said, "How is it that thou wilt manifest thyself to us, and not unto the world?" O Lord! said he, "I wish it were for everybody. I wish it were : my benevolence bids me wish it." Ah! my beloved, we never need be more benevolent than God is. Some say, "If all sinners were saved it would glorify God more." Certainly God knows better than we do how many sinners will glorify him, and we had better leave the number to him, and not get meddling with what we have no business with. It says in Scripture, "Fools will be meddling;" and fools they are who go meddling with what is no concern of theirs. But however this was, Judas said, "Lord, how is it that thou wilt manifest thyself unto us, and not unto the world?" Perhaps, again, it was *love to his Master* that made him put the question. "O Lord, I thought thou wouldst come and be king over all the world ; and now it appears that thou art only to be king over some." He wished Christ's dominion might be universal ; he wanted to see every heart the Saviour's throne, he desired every one to bow to him, and a very just and laudable wish it was; and so he asked Christ, "How can it be, Lord, that thou wilt not conquer all?" Jesus never answered the question. It was right to ask it ; but we shall never get the solution of it till we get up yonder ; perhaps not there. Yet again : perhaps the question was proposed by *admiration.* "Oh!" he said, "how is it that thou wilt manifest to *us,* and not unto the world?" Why, he might have said of himself, "What am I? What is my brother Peter here? Nothing but a fisherman. What is John? Nothing but a fisherman. And as for Matthew, he was a publican, and cheated hundreds. And Zaccheus, how many widows' houses did he devour! And yet 'thou sayest thou wilt manifest thyself unto us, and not unto the world.' There stands Mary the sinner : what did she do, that thou shouldst manifest thyself to her? And there is Mary Magdalene : she had seven devils. 'Lord, how is it that thou wilt manifest thyself unto *us* and not unto the world?'" Is not this a question we have often had to ask of our own souls?

> "Pause, my soul, adore and wonder;
> Ask, O why such love to me?"

And the only answer we could give was,

> "Grace hath put me in the number
> Of the Saviour's family."

Come to me and ask me, "Sir, why am I a Christian? Why does God love me?" I must reply "Because he does love you." "But why does he love me?" The only answer I can give you again is, "Because he would love you." For it is written, "He will have mercy on whom he will have mercy. Surely we might admiringly stand here and say, "Lord, why, Lord, why dost thou manifest thyself unto us, and not unto the world?" "Yes," but some would say, "because ye are better than the world; that is the reason." A fine lot better by nature, certainly! Better than the world by nature? Why, some of us were rather worse. There are some of you here who indulged once in every form of vice; who would blush to stand up here, and tell the sins you have committed. But God has manifested himself to you as he does not unto the world. Surely we shall have a perpetual cause of wonder in the doings of sovereign grace.

But *what is the answer?* Why does Christ manifest himself to some as he does not unto the world? The question was not answered; for it was unanswerable. Our Lord went on to say—"If a man love me, he will keep my words: and my Father will love him, and we will come unto him, and make our abode with him." He did not tell him why he would manifest himself unto them, and not unto the world. I have often been asked this question myself; "You say God manifests himself to some, and not to others—can you tell me why?" Well, Jesus Christ did not, and I cannot be expected to do it, any more than he did. But I will ask you whether you have any objection to it. Is it not enough that he should do so? He has declared that has he "power over the clay, to make of the same lump one vessel unto honor and another unto dishonor;" and if any one finds fault he saith, "Who art thou, O man? Shall the thing formed say to him that formed it, why hast thou made me thus?" What man shall ask of his father, "Why hast thou begotten me?" "Am I not God, and can I not do what I will with my own?" "But," says the objector, "is it not unjust for God to manifest himself to one and not to the other?" God replies: "Dost thou charge me with injustice? In what respect? Do I owe thee anything? Bring the bill and I will pay it. Do I owe you grace? Then grace would not be grace; it would be a debt. If I owe you grace, you shall have it." "But why should my brother have it? He is equally as bad as I." "Surely," replies the king, "I may give as I please." Thou hast two beggars at thy door: hast thou not a right to turn one away, and give the other something? And can I not do as I will with my own? "I will have mercy upon whom I will have mercy, and to whom I will give it." "Well," says the objector, "suppose I ask and plead for it, shall I not have it? "Yes, thou shalt," says God, for so the promise runs—"Every one that asketh receiveth, and he that seeketh findeth, and to him that knocketh it shall be opened." "But I cannot have it unless it is written that I shall have it." "Yes, but if thou askest, it is written that thou shalt ask; and the means are as much ordained as the end; thou couldst not ask unless I inclined thee, and now do not talk to me of injustice. I ask you to find the passage in my word where I ever promised to give grace to every one. Vile wretch! hast thou not rebelled against me? Thy doom is to be sent to hell for ever. Dost thou not deserve it?" "Yes." "Then who art thou that darest to accuse me of injustice? If I have fifty men on a scaffold to be hanged, have I not a right to pardon which I will, and give the punishment to all the rest? Wilt thou not yield to it?" "No," says the objector, "I will never yield to it." "Then, my friend expect not salvation till thou dost." Is there a man here who kicks against divine sovereignty? It is a testing doctrine; and if he does not receive it, it shows that his pride is not out of him. If we do but preach divine sovereignty, some will say, "That man is an Antinomian and a hyper." We disdain your slander, and remind you that the accusation might more properly be made against yourself. It is you that are the Antinomian, in rebelling against divine sovereignty. But a man who receives the doctrine of sovereignty will go to the throne, saying,

> " Perhaps he will admit my plea,
>   Perhaps will hear my prayer:
> But if I perish I will pray,
>   And perish only there."

And now, what say you to this, my friends? I know what some would say. They would cry, "Nonsense! we believe religion is a thing very good to keep people in order; but as to these manifestations and these ecstacies, we do not believe in them." Very well, beloved, I have just proved the truth of what the text says. He does not manifest himself unto the world; and you have proved yourself that you are one of the world, because you have not any manifestations. But there are some Christians here who say, "We do not know much about these manifestations." No, I know you do not. The church has been getting for the last few years into a lean, starved state; God has sent very few preachers who would preach up these special things, and the church has been getting lower and lower; and what would become of us I cannot tell, if there were not saved a little salt, which God has scattered over the putrifying mass. Some of us have been living on low ground, when we might have been standing on high places; We have been tarrying in the valley of Baca, when we might as well have been living on the top of Carmal. I would not choose to dwell in a valley, if I might build my house on the delectable mountains. O Christian! up this morning! Let thy feet be shod with light once more; trip lightly across the plain of trouble; get to the side of Calvary; ascend to the very summit; and from Calvary I tell thee, thou canst see across the plain as far ash eaven itself. If thou canst but get to Pisgah's top, thou shalt sing,

> " Sweet fields beyond the swelling flood
>   Stand dressed in living green.

And your spirit shall become like the chariots of Amminadib. Seek, my brethren such spiritual manifestations, if you have never experienced them; and if ye have been privileged to enjoy them, seek more of them; for what is there can so certainly make life happy, and so fit you for the sky, as these revelations of Jesus Christ? Oh! ye who despise what *we* enjoy, from the depths of my soul I pity you. Take heed, lest the first revelation you have of Christ be, when he shall be revealed in flaming fire, taking vengeance on his enemies; for if he is not revealed in mercy, he will be in justice. God give you grace to see him on Calvary before you see him on Sinai; to behold him as the Saviour of sinners, before you see him as the judge of quick and dead. God bless you, and lead you to seek these manifestations constantly! Amen.

The Glorious Habitation.

"Lord, thou hast been our dwelling place in all generations."—Psalm xc. 1.

MOSES was the inspired author of three devotional compositions. We first of all find him as Moses the poet, singing the song which is aptly joined with that of Jesus, in the Revelation, where it says, "The song of Moses and of the Lamb." He was a poet on the occasion when Pharaoh and his hosts were cast into the Red Sea, "his chosen captains also were drowned in the Red Sea." Further on in his life we discover him in the character of a preacher; and then his doctrine distilled as the dew, and his speech dropped like the rain, in those chapters which are full of glorious imagery, and rich with poetry, which you will find in the Book of Deuteronomy. And now in the Psalms, we find him the author of a prayer: "A prayer of Moses, the man of God." Happy combination of the poet, the preacher, and the man of prayer! Where three such things are found together, the man becomes a very giant above his fellows. It often happens that the man who preaches has but little poetry; and the man who is the poet would not be able to preach and utter his poems before immense assemblies, but would be only fit to write them by himself. It is a rare combination when true devotion and the spirit of poetry and eloquence meet in the same man. You will see in this Psalm a wondrous depth of spirituality; you will mark how the poet subsides into the man of God; and how, lost in himself, he sings his own frailty, declares the glory of God, and asks that he may have the blessing of his heavenly Father always resting on his head.

This first verse will derive peculiar interest if you remember the place where Moses was when he thus prayed. He was in the wilderness; not in some of the halls of Pharaoh, nor yet in a habitation in the land of Goshen, but in a wilderness. And perhaps from the summit of the hill, looking upon the tribes of Israel as they were taking up their tents and marching along, he thought, "Ah! poor travellers, they seldom rest anywhere; they have not any settled habitation where they can dwell. Here they have no continuing city;" but he lifted his eyes above, and he said, "Lord, thou hast been our dwelling place in all generations." Passing his eye back through history, he saw one great temple where God's people had dwelt; and with his prophetical eye rolling with sacred frenzy, he could foresee that throughout all futurity the specially chosen of God would be able to sing, "Lord, thou hast been our dwelling place in all generations."

Taking this verse as the subject of our discourse this morning, we shall, first of all, *explain it;* and then we shall try and do what the old Puritans called "*improve*" it; by which they did not mean improve the text, but improve the people a little by the consideration of the verse.

I. First we will try to explain it somewhat. Here is *a habitation:* "Lord, thou hast been our dwelling place;" and, secondly, if I may use such a common word, here is *the lease of it:* "Thou hast been our dwelling place in all generations."

First, then, here is *a habitation:* "Lord, thou hast been our habitation." The mighty Jehovah, who filleth all immensity, the Eternal, Everlasting, Great I Am, does not refuse to allow figures concerning himself. Though he is so high that the eye of angel hath not seen him, though he is so lofty that the wing of cherub hath not reached him, though he is so great that the utmost extent of the travels of immortal spirits have never discovered the limit of himself—yet he does not object

31

that his people should speak of him thus familiarly, and should say, 'Jehovah, thou hast been our dwelling place." We shall understand this figure better by contrasting the thought, with the state of Israel in the wilderness; and secondly, by making mention of some things by way of comparison, which are peculiar to our house, and which we never can enjoy if we are not the possessors of a dwelling place of our own.

First, we shall contrast this thought, "Lord, thou hast been our dwelling place," with the peculiar position of the Israelites as they were travelling through the wilderness.

We remark, first, that *they must have been in a state of great uneasiness.* At nightfall or when the pillar stayed its motion, the tents were pitched, and they laid themselves down to rest. Perhaps on the morrow, ere the morning sun had risen, the trumpet sounded, they stirred themselves from their beds and found the ark was in motion, and the fiery, cloudy pillar was leading the way through the narrow defiles of the mountain up the hill side, or along the arid waste of the wilderness. They had scarcely time to arrange their little property in their tents and make all things comfortable for themselves, before they heard the sound of "Away! away! away! this is not your rest; you must still be onward journeying towards Canaan!" They could not plant a little patch of ground around their tent, they could not lay out their house in order, and arrange their furniture, they could not become attached to the spot of ground. Even though just now their father had been buried in a place where a tent had tarried for a time; yet they must be off. They must have no attachment to the place, they must have nothing of what we call comfort, ease, and peace, but be always journeying, always travelling. Moreover, so exposed were they, that they never could be very easy in their tents. At one time the sand, with the hot simoom behind it, would drive through the tent and cover them almost to burial. On frequent occasions the hot sun would scorch them, and their canvas would scarce be a preservation; at another time the biting north wind would freeze around them, so that within their tents they sat shivering and cowering around their fires. They had little ease; but behold the contrast which Moses, the Man of God, discerns with gratitude, "Thou art not our tent, but thou art our dwelling place. Though we are uneasy here, though we are tossed from side to side by troubles, though we travel through a wilderness, and find it a rough pathway, though when we sit down here we know not what comfort means; O Lord, in thee we possess all the comforts which a house can afford, we have all that a mansion or palace can give the prince, who can loll upon his couch, and rest upon his bed of down. Lord, thou art to us comfort, thou art a house and habitation." Have you ever known what it is to have God for your dwelling place in the sense of comfort? Do you know what it is, when you have storms behind you, to feel like a sea-bird, blown to the land by the very storm? Do you know what it is, when you have been caged sometimes by adversity, to have the string cut by divine grace, and like the pigeon that flies at once to its own dovecot, have you sped your way across the ether, and found yourself in God? Do you know what it is, when you are tossed on the waves, to go down into the depths of Godhead, there rejoicing that not a wave of trouble ruffles your spirit, but that you are serenely at home with God your own Almighty Father? Can you amidst all the uneasiness of this desert journey find a comfort there? Is the breast of Jesus a sweet pillow for your head? Can you lie thus on the breast of Deity? Can you put yourself on the stream of Providence and float along without a struggle, while angels sing around you—divinely guided, divinely led—" We are bearing thee along the stream of Providence to the ocean of eternal bliss!" Do you know what it is to lie on God, to give up all care, to drive anxiety away, and there—not in a recklessness of spirit, but in a holy carelessness—to be careful for nothing, "but in everything by supplication to make known your wants unto God?" If so, ye have gained the first idea: "Lord, thou hast been our dwelling place throughout all generations."

Again, the Israelites were *very much exposed to all kinds of noxious creatures*, owing to their residing in tents, and their habits of wandering. At one time the fiery serpent was their foe. By night the wild beasts prowled around them. Unless that fiery pillar had been a wall of fire around them and a glory in the midst, they might all have fallen a prey to the wild monsters that roamed the deserts. Worse foes they found in human kind. The Amalekites rushed down from the mountains, wild wandering hordes constantly attacked them. They never felt themselves secure, for they were travellers through an enemy's country. They were hasting across a land where they were not wanted, to another land that was providing means to oppose them when they should arrive. Such is the Christian. He is journeying through an enemy's land, every day he is exposed to danger. His tent may be broken down by death; the slanderer is behind him, the open foeman is before him; the wild beast that prowls by night, and the pestilence that wasteth by day, continually seek his destruction; he finds no rest where he is; he feels himself exposed. But, says Moses, "Though we live in a tent exposed to wild beasts and fierce men, yet thou art our habitation. In thee we find no exposure. Within thee we find ourselves secure, and in thy glorious person we dwell as in an impregnable tower of defence, safe from every fear and alarm, knowing that we are secure." O Christian, hast thou ever known what it is to stand in the midst of battles, with arrows flying thick around thee more than thy shield can catch ; and yet thou hast been as secure as if thou wert folding thine arms and resting within the walls of some strong bastion, where arrow could not reach thee, and where even the sound of trumpet could not disturb thine ears ? Hast thou known what it is to dwell securely in God, to enter into the Most High, and laugh to scorn the anger, the frowns, the sneers, the contempt, the slander and calumny of men; to ascend into the sacred place of the pavilion of the Most High, and to abide under the shadow of the Almighty, and to feel thyself secure ? And mark thee, thou mayest do this. In times of pestilence it is possible to walk in the midst of cholera and death, singing—

> "Plagues and deaths around me fly,
> Till he please, I cannot die."

It is possible to stand exposed to the utmost degree of danger, and yet to feel such a holy serenity that we can laugh at fear; too great, too mighty, too powerful through God to stoop for one moment to the cowardice of trembling: "we know whom we have believed, and we are persuaded that he is able to keep that which we have committed unto him." When houseless men wander, when poor distressed spirits, beaten by the storm, find no refuge, we enter into God, and shutting behind us the door of faith, we say, "Howl ye winds, blow ye tempests, roar ye wild beasts, come on ye robbers!

> ' He that hath made his refuge God
> Shall find a most secure abode,
> Shall walk all day beneath his shade,
> And there at night shall rest his head.'"

Lord, in this sense, thou hast been our habitation.

Again, poor Israel in the wilderness *were continually exposed to change.* They were never in one place long. Sometimes they might tarry for a month in one spot—just near the seventy palm trees. What a sweet and pleasant place to go out each morning, to sit beside the well and drink that clear stream! "Onward!" cries Moses; and he takes them to a place where the bare rocks stand out from the mountain side, and the red burning sand is beneath their feet; vipers spring up around them, and thorny brakes grow instead of pleasing vegetation. What a change have they! Yet, another day they shall come to a place that shall be more dreary still. They walk through a defile so close and narrow, that the affrighted rays of the sun dare scarce enter such a prison, lest they should ne'er find their way out again! They must go onward from place to place, continually changing, never having time to settle, and to say, "Now we are secure, in this place we shall dwell." Here, again, the contrast casts light upon the text—"Ah!" says Moses, "though we are always changing, Lord, thou hast been our dwelling place throughout all generations." The Christian knows no change with regard to God. He may be rich to-day and poor to-morrow; he may be sickly to-day and well to-morrow; he may be in happiness to day, to-morrow he may be distressed; but there is no change with regard to his relationship to God. If he loved me yesterday he loves me to-day. I am neither better nor worse in God than I ever was. Let prospects be blighted, let hopes be blasted, let joy be withered, let mildews destroy everything, I have lost nothing of what I have in God. He is my strong habitation whereunto I can continually resort. The Christian never becomes poorer, and never grows

33

richer with regard to God. "Here," he can say, "is a thing that never can pass away or change. On the brow of the Eternal there is ne'er a furrow; his hair is unwhitened by age; his arm is unpalsied by weakness; his heart does not change in its affections; his will does not vary in its purpose; he is the Immutable Jehovah, standing fast and for ever. Thou art our habitation! As the house changes not, but stands in the same place, so have I found thee from my youth up. When first I was cast upon thee from my mother's breast I found thee my God of Providence. When first I knew thee by that spiritual knowledge which thou alone canst give, I found thee a sure habitation; and I find thee such now. Yea, when I shall be old and grey-headed, I know thou wilt not forsake me; thou wilt be the same dwelling place in all generations."

One thought more in contrasting the position of the Israelites with ourselves,—that is *weariness*. How weary must Israel have been in the wilderness! how tired must have been the soles of their feet with their constant journeyings! They were not in a place of repose, luxury, and rest, but in a land of journeying, and weariness, and trouble. I think I see them travelling, wiping frequently the burning sweat from their brows, and saying, "Oh! that we had a habitation where we might rest! Oh! that we could enter a land of vines and Pomegranates, a city where we might enjoy immunity from alarm! God has promised it to us, but we have not found it. There remaineth a rest for the people of God: O that we might find it." Christian! God is your habitation in this sense. He is your rest; and you will never find rest except in him. I defy a man who has no God to have a soul at rest. He who has not Jesus for his Saviour, will always be a restless spirit. Read some of Byron's verses, and you will find him (if he was truly picturing himself) to be the very personification of that spirit who "walked to and fro, seeking rest and finding none." Here is one of his verses—

> "I fly like a bird of the air,
>   In search of a home and a rest;
> A balm for the sickness of care,
>   A bliss for a bosom unblest."

Read the lives of any men who have had no gospel justification, or have had no knowledge of God, and you will find that they were like the poor bird that had its nest pulled down, and knew not where to rest, flying about, wandering, and seeking a habitation. Some of you have tried to find rest out of God. You have sought to find it in your wealth; but you have pricked your head when you have laid it on that pillow. You have sought it in a friend, but that friend's arm has been a broken reed, where you hoped it would be a wall of strength. You will never find rest except in God; there is no refuge but in him. Oh! what rest and composures are there in him! It is more than sleep, more than calm, more than quiet; deeper than the dead stillness of the noiseless sea in its utmost depths, where it is undisturbed by the slightest ripple, and winds can never intrude. There is a holy calm and sweet repose which the Christian only knows, something like the slumbering stars up there in beds of azure; or like the seraphic rest which we may suppose beatified spirits have when they before the throne continually bow—there is a rest so deep and calm, so still and quiet, so profound, that we find no works to describe it. You have tried it, and can rejoice in it. You know that the Lord has been your dwelling place—your sweet, calm, constant home, where you can enjoy peace in all generations. But I have dwelt too long upon this part of the subject, and I will speak of it in a different way.

First of all, *the dwelling place of man is the place where he can unbend himself, and feel himself at home, and speak familiarly*. In this pulpit I must somewhat check my words; I deal with men of the world who watch my speech, and are ever on the catch, men who wish to have this or that to retail—I must be on my guard. So you men of business, when you are on the exchange, or in your shop, have to guard yourselves. What does the man do at home? He can lay bare his breast, and do, and say as he pleases: it is his own house—his dwelling place; and is he not master there? shall he not do as he will with his own? Assuredly; for he feels himself at home. Ah! my beloved, do you ever find yourself in God to be at home? Have you been with Christ, and told your secrets in his ear, and found that you could do

34

so without reserve? We do not generally tell secrets to other people, for if we do, and make them promise that they will never tell them, they *will* never tell them except to the first person they meet. Most persons who have secrets told them, are like the lady of whom it is said she never told her secrets except to two sorts of persons—those that asked her, and those that did not. You must not trust men of the world; but do you know what it is to tell all your secrets to God in prayer, to whisper all your thoughts to him? You are not ashamed to confess your sins to him with all their aggravations; you make no apologies to God, but you put in every aggravation, you describe all the depths of your baseness. Then, as for your little wants, you would be ashamed to tell them to another: before God you can tell them all. You can tell him your grief that you would not whisper to your dearest friend. With God you can be always at home; you need be under no restraint. The Christian at once give God the key of his heart, and lets him turn everything over. He says, "There is the key of every cabinet; it is my desire that thou wouldst open them all. If there are jewels, they are thine; and if there be things that should not be there, drive them out. Search me, and try my heart." The more God lives in the Christian, the better the Chriscian loves him; the oftener God comes to see him, the better he loves his God. And God loves his people all the more when they are familiar with him. Can you say in this sense, "Lord, thou hast been my dwelling place."

Then again, *man's home is the place where his affections are centred.* God deliver us from those men who do not love their homes! Lives there a man so base, so dead, that he has no affection for his own house? If so, surely the spark of Christianity must have died entirely out. It is *natural* that men should love their homes; it is *spiritual* that they should love them better still. In our homes we find those to whom we must and ever shall be most attached. There our best friends and kindred dwell. When we wander, we are as birds that have left their nests and can find no settled home. We wish to go back, and to see again that smile, to grasp once more that loving hand, and to find that we are with those to whom the ties of affection have knit us. We wish to feel—and every Christian man will feel—with regard to his own family, that they are the warp and woof of his own nature, that he has become a part and portion of them; and there he centres his affection. He cannot afford to lavish his love everywhere. He centres it in that particular spot, that oasis in this dark desert world. Christian man, is God your habitation in that sense? Have you given your whole soul to God? do you feel you can bring your whole heart to him, and say, "O God! I love from my soul; with the most impassioned earnestness I love thee.

> ' The dearest idol I have known—
> Whate'er that idol be—
> Help me to tear it from its throne,
> And worship only thee!

O God! though I sometimes wander, yet I love thee in my wanderings, and my heart is fixed on thee. What though the creature doth beguile me, I detest that creature; it is to me as the apple of Sodom. Thou art the master of my soul, the emperor of my heart; no vice-regent, but king of kings. My spirit is fixed on thee as the centre of my soul.

> ' Thou art the sea of love
> Where all my pleasures roll,
> The circle where my passions move;
> The centre of my soul.'

O God! thou has been our dwelling place in all generations."

My next remark is concerning the *lease of this dwelling place.* God is the believer's habitation. Sometimes, you know, people get turned out of their houses, or their houses tumble down about their ears. It is never so with ours; God is our dwelling place throughout all generations. Let us look back in times past, and we shall find that God has been our habitation. Oh, the old house at home! who does not love it, the place of our childhood, the old roof tree, the old cottage! There is no village in all the world half so good as that particular village where we were born! True, the gates, and stiles, and posts have been altered; but still there is an attachment to those old houses, the old tree in the park, and the old ivy-mantled tower. It is not very picturesque, perhaps, but we love to go to see it. We like to see the haunts of our boyhood. There is something pleasant in those old stairs where the clock used to stand; and in the room where grandmother was wont to bend her knee, and where we had family prayer. There is no place like that house after all! Well, beloved, God has been the habitation of the Christian in years that are gone by. Christian, your house is indeed a venerable house, and you have long dwelt there. You dwelt there in the person of Christ long before you were brought into this sinful world; and it is to be your dwelling place throughout all generations. You are never to ask for another house; you will always be contented with that one you have; you will never wish to change your habitation. And if you wished it you could not, for he is your dwelling place in all generations. God give you to know what it is to take this house in its long lease, and ever to have God for your dwelling place!

II. Now I come to improve this text somewhat. First, let us improve it to SELF-EXAMINATION. How may we know whether we be Christians or not, whether the Lord is our dwelling place, and will be throughout all generations? I shall give you some hints for self-examination, by referring you to several passages which I have looked out in the first epistle of John. It is remarkable that almost the only Scriptural writer who speaks of God as a dwelling place, is that most loving apostle, John, out of whose epistle we have been reading.

He gives us in the 12th verse of the 4th chapter, one means of knowing whether we are living in God: "*If we love another*, God dwelleth in us, and his love is perfected in us." And again, further on, he says, "And we have known and believed the love that God hath to us. God is love; and he that dwelleth in love dwelleth in God, and God in him." You may then tell whether you are a tenant of this great spiritual house by the love you have towards others. Have you a love towards the saints? Well, then you are a saint yourself. The goats will not love the sheep; and if you love the sheep, it is an evidence that you are a sheep yourself. Many of the Lord's weak family never can get any other evidences of their conversion except this—"We know that we have passed from death unto life, because we love the brethren." And though that is a very little evidence, yet it is such a one that the strongest faith often cannot get a much better. "If I do not love God, I love his people; if I am not a Christian, I love his house." What! has the devil told thee thou art not the Lord's Poor Faintheart, dost thou love the Lord's people? "Yes," sayest thou, "I love to see their faces and to hear their prayers; I could almost kiss the hem of their garments." Is it so? and would you give to them if they were poor? would you visit them if they were sick, and tend them if they needed assistance? "Ah! yes." Then fear not. You who love God's people must love the Master. We know we dwell in God if we love one another.

In the 13th verse is another sign: "Hereby know we that we dwell in him, and he in us, because *he hath given us of his Spirit*." Have we ever had the Spirit of God in us? That is one of the most solemn questions I can ask. Many of you know what it is to be excited by religious feeling who never had the Spirit of God. Many of us have great need to tremble lest we should not have received that Spirit. I have tried myself scores of times, in different ways, to see whether I really am a possessor of the Spirit of God or not. I know that the people of the world scoff at the idea, and say, "It is impossible for anybody to have the Spirit of God." Then it is impossible for anybody to go to heaven; for we must have the Spirit of God, we must be born again of the Spirit, before we can enter there. What a serious question is this: "Have I had the Spirit of God in me?" True, my soul is at times lifted on high, and I feel that I could sing like a seraph. True, sometimes I am melted down by deep devotion, and I could pray in terrible solemnity. But so could hypocrites, perhaps. Have I the Spirit of God? Have you any evidence within you that you have the Spirit? Are you sure that you are not labouring under a delusion and a dream? Have you actually the Spirit of God within you? If so, you dwell in God. That is the second sign.

But the apostle gives another sign in the 15th verse: "Whosoever shall *confess that Jesus is the Son of God*, God dwelleth in him, and he in God." The confession of our faith in the Saviour is another sign that we live in God. Oh! poor heart, canst thou not come under this sign? Thou mayest have but little boldness, but

36

canst thou not say, "I believe in the name of the Lord Jesus Christ?" If so, thou dwellest in God. Many of you, I know, say, "When I hear a sermon I feel affected by it. When I am in the House of God I feel like a child of God, but the business, cares, and troubles of life take me off, and then I fear I am not." But you can say, "I do believe in Christ; I know I cast myself on his mercy, and hope to be saved by him." Then do not say you are not a child of God if you have faith.

But there is one more sign whereby we ought to examine ourselves, in the 3rd chap. 24th verse: "*He that keepeth his commandments dwelleth in him,* and he in him." Obedience to the commandments of God is a blessed sign of a dwelling in God. Some of you have a deal of religious talk, but not much religious walk; a large stock of outside piety, but not much real inward piety, which develops itself in your actions. That is a hint for some of you who know that it is right to be baptized, and are not. You know it is one of the commandments of God, that "he that believeth shall be baptized," and you are neglecting what you know to be your duty. You are dwelling in God, I doubt not, but you lack one evidence of it, namely—obedience to God's commandments. Obey God, and then you will know that you are dwelling in him.

But I have another word by way of improvement. and that is one of CONGRATULA-TION. You who dwell in God, allow me to congratulate you. Thrice happy men are ye, if ye are dwelling in God! You need not blush to compare yourselves with angels; you need not think that any on earth can share such happiness as yours! Zion, oh, how blessed art thou, freed from all sins! Now thou art, through Christ, made to dwell in God, and therefore art eternally secure! I congratulate you, Christians, first, that you have such a *magnificent house* to dwell in. You have not a palace that shall be as gorgeous as Solomon's,—a mighty palace as immense as the dwellings of the kings of Assyria, or Babylon; but you have a God that is more than mortal creatures can behold; you dwell in an immortal fabric, you dwell in the Godhead—something which is beyond all human skill. I congratulate, moreover, that you live in such a *perfect house.* There ne'er was a house on earth that could not be made a little better; but the house you dwell in has everything you want; in God you have all you require. I congratulate you, moreover, that you live in a house that shall *last for ever;* a dwelling place that shall not pass away. When this world shall have been scattered like a dream; when, like the bubble on the breaker, creation shall have died away; when all this universe shall have died out like a spark from an expiring brand, your house shall live and stand more imperishable than marble, more solid than granite, self-existent as God, for it is God! Be happy then.

Now, lastly, a word of ADMONITION AND WARNING to some of you. My hearers, what a pity it is that we have to divide our congregation; that we cannot speak to you in a mass as being all Christians. This morning, I would I could take God's Word and address it to you all, that you all might share the sweet promises it contains. But some of you would not have them if I were to offer them. Some of you despise Christ, my blessed Master. Many of you think sin to be a trifle, and grace to be worthless; heaven to be a vision, and hell to be a fiction. Some of you are careless, and hardened, and thoughtless, without God, and without Christ. Oh! my hearers, I wonder at myself that I should have so little benevolence, that I do not preach more fervently to you. Methinks if I could get a right estimate of your souls' value that I should not speak as I do now, with stammering tongue, but with flaming words. I have great cause to blush at my own slothfulnes, though God knows I have striven to preach God's truth as vehemently as possible, and would spend myself in his service; but I wonder I do not stand in every street in London and preach his truth. When I think of the thousands of souls in this great city that have never heard of Jesus, that have never listened to him; when I think of how much ignorance exists, and how little gospel preaching there is, how few souls are saved, I think—O God! what little grace I must have, that I do not strive more for souls.

One word by way of *warning.* Do you know, poor soul, that you have not a house to live in? You have a house for your body but no house for your soul. Have you ever seen a poor girl at midnight sitting down on a door step crying? Somebody passes by, and says, "Why do you sit here?" "I have no house, sir; I have no home." "Where is your father?" "My father's dead, sir." "Where is your mother?" "I have no mother, sir." "Have you no friends?" "No friends at all." "Have you no house?" "No; I have none. I am houseless." And she shivers in the chill air, and gathers her poor ragged shawl around her, and cries again, "I have no house—I have no home." Would you not pity her? Would you blame her for her tears? Ah! there are some of you that have houseless souls here this morning. It is something to have a houseless body; but to think of a houseless soul! Methinks I see you in eternity sitting on the door-step of heaven. An angel says, "What! have you no house to live in?" "No house," says the poor soul. "Have you no father?" "No; God is not my father; and there is none beside him." "Have you no mother?" "No; the church is not my mother; I never sought her ways, nor loved Jesus. I have neither father nor mother." "Have you no house then?" "No; I am a houseless soul." But there is one thing worse about that—houseless souls have to be sent into hell; to a dungeon, to a lake that burns with fire. Houseless soul! in a little while thy body will have gone; and where wilt thou house thyself when the hot hail of eternal vengeance comes from heaven? Where wilt thou hide thy guilty head, when the winds of the last judgment day shall sweep on thee with fury? Where wilt thou shelter thyself when the blast of the terrible one shall be as a storm against a wall, when the darkness of eternity comes upon thee, and hell thickens round thee? It will be all in vain for you to cry, "Rocks, hide me; mountains, fall upon me"—the rocks will not obey you, the mountains will not hide you. Caverns would be palaces if you could dwell in them, but there will be no caverns for you to hide your head in, but you will be houseless souls, houseless spirits, wandering through the shades of hell, tormented, destitute, afflicted, and that throughout eternity. Poor houseless soul, dost thou want a house? I have a house to let this morning for every sinner who feels his misery. Do you want a house for your soul? Then I will condescend to men of low estate, and tell you in homely language, that I have a house to let. Do you ask me what is the purchase? I will tell you; it is something less than proud human nature will like to give. It is without money and without price. Ah! you would like to pay some rent wouldn't you? You would love to do something to win Christ. You cannot have the house then; it is "without money and without price." I have told you enough of the house itself, and therefore I will not describe its excellencies. But I will tell you one thing—that if you feel you are a houseless soul this morning, you may have the key to-morrow; and if you feel yourself to be a houseless soul to-day, you may enter it now. If you had a house of your own I would not offer it to you; but since you have no other, here it is. Will you take my Master's house on a lease for all eternity, with nothing to pay for it, nothing but the ground-rent of loving and serving him for ever? Will you take Jesus, and dwell in him throughout eternity, or will you be content to be a houseless soul? Come inside, sir; see, it is furnished from top to bottom with all you want. It has cellars filled with gold, more than you will spend as long as you live; it hath a parlor where you can entertain yourself with Christ, and feast on his love; it has tables well stored with food for you to live on for ever; it hath a drawing-room of brotherly love where you can receive your friends. You will find a resting room up there where you can rest with Jesus; and on the top there is a look-out, whence you can see heaven itself. Will you have the house, or will you not? Ah, if you are houseless, you will say, "I should like to have the hovse; but may I have it?" Yes; there is the key. The key is, "Come to Jesus." But you say "I am too shabby for such a house." Never mind; there are garments inside. As Rowland Hill once said—

> "Come naked, come filthy, come ragged, come poor,
> Come wretched, come dirty, come just as you are."

If you feel guilty and condemned, come, and though the house is too good for you, Christ will make you good enough for the house by-and-bye. He will wash you, and cleanse you, and you will yet be able to sing with Moses, with the same unfaltering voice, "Lord, thou hast been *my* dwelling place throughout all generations."

———

A Jealous God

"For the Lord, whose name is jealous, is a jealous God."—Exodus xxxiv. 14.

THE passion of jealousy in man is usually exercised in an evil manner, but it is not in itself necessarily sinful. A man may be zealously cautious of his honour, and suspiciously vigilant over another, without deserving blame. All thoughtful persons will agree that there is such a thing as virtuous jealousy. Self-love is, no doubt, the usual foundation of human jealousy, and it may be that Shenstone is right in his definition of it as "the apprehension of superiority," the fear lest another should by any means supplant us; yet the word "*jealous*" is so near akin to that noble word "*zealous*," that I am persuaded it must have something good in it. Certainly we learn from Scripture that there is such a thing as a godly jealousy. We find the Apostle Paul declaring to the Corinthian Church, "I am jealous over you with a godly jealousy, for I have espoused you to one husband that I may present you as a chaste virgin to Christ." He had an earnest, cautious, anxious concern for their holiness, that the Lord Jesus might be honoured in their lives. Let it be remembered then, that jealousy, like anger, is not evil in itself, or it could never be ascribed to God; his jealousy is ever a pure and holy flame. The passion of jealousy possesses an intense force, it fires the whole nature, its coals are juniper, which have a most vehement flame ; it resides in the lowest depths of the heart, and takes so firm a hold that it remains most deeply rooted until the exciting cause is removed ; it wells up from the inmost recesses of the nature, and like a torrent irresistibly sweeps all before it ; it stops at nothing, for it is cruel as the grave (Cant. viii. 6), it provokes wrath to the utmost, for it is the rage of a man, therefore he will not spare in the day of vengeance (Prov. vi. 34), and it overthrows everything in the pursuit of its enemy, for "wrath is cruel, and anger is outrageous ; but who is able to stand before jealousy ?" For all these reasons jealousy is selected as some faint picture of that tender regard which God has for His own Deity, honour, and supremacy, and the holy indignation which he feels towards those who violate his laws, offend his majesty, or impeach his character. Not that God is jealous so as to bring him down to the likeness of men, but that this is the nearest idea we can form of what the Divine Being feels—if it be right to use even that word toward him—when he beholds his throne occupied by false gods, his dignity insulted, and his glory usurped by others. We cannot speak of God except by using figures drawn from his works, or our own emotions; we ought, however, when we use the images, to caution ourselves and those who listen to us, against the idea that the Infinite mind is really to be compassed and described by any metaphors however lofty, or language however weighty. We might not have ventured to use the word, "jealousy" in connection with the Most High, but as we find it so many times in Scripture, let us with solemn awe survey this mysterious display of the Divine mind. Methinks I hear the thundering words of Nahum, "God is jealous and the Lord revengeth, the Lord revengeth and is furious, the Lord will take vengeance on his adversaries, and he reserveth wrath for his enemies." My soul be thou humbled before the Lord and tremble at his name!

(I.) Reverently, let us remember that the LORD IS EXCEEDINGLY JEALOUS OF HIS DEITY.

Our text is coupled with the command—"Thou shalt worship no other God." When the law was thundered from Sinai, the second commandment received force from the divine jealousy—"Thou shalt not make unto thee any graven image, or any likeness of anything that is in the heaven above, or that is in the earth beneath, or that is in the water under the earth; Thou shalt not bow down thyself to them, nor serve them: for I the Lord thy God am a jealous God." Since he is the only God, the Creator of heaven and earth, he cannot endure that any creature of his own hands, or fiction of a creature's imagination should be thrust into his throne, and be made to wear his crown. In Ezekiel we find the false god described as "the image of jealousy which provoketh to jealousy," and the doom on Jerusalem for thus turning from Jehovah runs thus, "Mine eye shall not spare, neither will I have pity, but I will recompense their way upon their head." False gods patiently endure the existence of other false gods. Dagon can stand with Bel, and Bel with Ashtaroth; how should stone, and wood, and silver, be moved to indignation; but because God is the only living and true God, Dagon must fall before his ark; Bel must be broken, and Ashtaroth must be consumed with fire. Thus saith the Lord, "Ye shall destroy their altars, break their images, and cut down their groves;" the idols he shall utterly abolish. My brethren, do you marvel at this? I felt in my own soul while meditating upon this matter an intense sympathy with God. Can you put yourselves in God's place for a moment? Suppose that you had made the heavens and the earth, and all the creatures that inhabit this round globe; how would you feel if those creatures should set up an image of wood, or brass, or gold, and cry, "These are the gods that made us; these things give us life." What—a dead piece of earth set up in rivalry with real Deity! What must be the Lord's indignation against infatuated rebels when they so far despise him as to set up a leek, or an onion, or a beetle, or a frog, preferring to worship the fruit of their own gardens, or the vermin of their muddy rivers, rather than acknowledge the God in whose hand their breath is, and whose are all their ways! Oh! it is a marvel that God hath not dashed the world to pieces with thunderbolts, when we recollect that even to this day millions of men have changed the glory of the incorruptible God into an image made like to corruptible man, and to birds and four-footed beasts, and creeping things. With what unutterable contempt must the living God look down upon those idols which are the work of man's hands—"They have mouths, but they speak not: eyes have they, but they see not: they have ears, but they hear not: noses have they, but they smell not: they have hands, but they handle not: feet have they, but they walk not: neither speak they through their throat." God hath longsuffering toward men, and he patiently endureth this madness of rebellion; but, oh! what patience must it be which can restrain the fury of his jealousy, for he is a jealous God, and brooks no rival. It was divine jealousy which moved the Lord to bring all his plagues on Egypt. Careful reading will shew you that those wonders were all aimed at the gods of Egypt. The people were tormented by the very things which they had made to be their deities, or else, as in the case of the murrain, their sacred animals were themselves smitten, even as the Lord had threatened—"Against all the gods of Egypt I will execute judgment: I am Jehovah." Was it not the same with ancient Israel? Why were they routed before their enemies? Why was their land so often invaded? Why did famine follow pestilence, and war succeed to famine? Only because "they provoked him to anger with their high places, and moved him to jealousy with their graven images. When God heard this, he was wroth, and greatly abhorred Israel." (Ps. lxxviii. 58, 59.) How was it that at the last the Lord gave up Jerusalem to the flames, and bade the Chaldeans carry into captivity the remnant of his people? How was it that he abhorred his heritage, and gave up Mount Zion to be trodden under foot by the Gentiles? Did not Jeremiah tell them plainly that because they had walked after other gods and forsaken Jehovah, therefore he would cast them out into a land which they knew not?

Brethren, the whole history of the human race is a record of the wars of the Lord against idolatry. The right hand of the Lord hath dashed in pieces the enemy and cast the ancient idols to the ground. Behold the heaps of Nineveh! Search for the desolations of Babylon! Look upon the broken temples of Greece! See the ruins of Pagan Rome! Journey where you will, you behold the dilapidated temples of the gods and the ruined empires of their foolish votaries. The moles and the bats have covered with forgetfulness the once famous deities of Chaldea and Assyria. The Lord hath made bare his arm and eased him of his adversaries, for Jehovah, whose name is Jealous, is a jealous God.

With what indignation, then, must the Lord look down upon that apostate harlot, called *the Romish Church*, when, in all her sanctuaries, there are pictures and images, relics and shrines, and poor infatuated beings are even taught to bow before a piece of bread. In this country, Popish idolatry is not so barefaced and naked as it is in other lands; but I have seen it, and my soul has been moved with indignation like that of Paul on Mars' Hill, when he saw the city wholly given to idolatry; I have seen thousands adore the wafer, hundreds bow before the image of the Virgin, scores at prayer before a crucifix, and companies of men and women adoring a rotten bone or a rusty nail, because said to be the relic of a saint. It is vain for the Romanist to assert that he worships not the things themselves, but only the Lord through them, for this the second commandment expressly forbids, and it is upon this point that the Lord calls himself a jealous God. How full is that cup which Babylon must drink; the day is hastening when the Lord shall avenge himself upon her, because her iniquities have reached unto heaven, and she hath blasphemously exalted her Pope into the throne of the Most High, and thrust her priests into the office of the Lamb. Purge yourselves, purge yourselves of this leaven. I charge you before God, the Judge of quick and dead, if ye would not be partakers of her plagues, come out from her more and more, and let your protest be increasingly vehement against this which exalteth itself above all that is called God. Let our Protestant Churches, which have too great a savour of Popery in them, cleanse themselves of her fornications, lest the Lord visit them with fire and pour the plagues of Babylon upon them. Renounce, my brethren, every ceremony which has not Scripture for its warrant, and every doctrine which is not established by the plain testimony of the Word of God. Let us, above all, never by any sign, or word, or deed, have any complicity with this communion of devils, this gathering together of the sons of Belial: and since our God is a jealous God, let us not provoke him by any affinity, gentleness, fellowship, or amity with this Mother of Harlots and abominations of the earth.

With what jealousy must the Lord regard the *great mass of the people of this country*, who have another God beside himself! With what indignation doth he look upon many of you who are subject to the prince of the power of the air, the god of this world! To you Jehovah is nothing. God is not in all your thoughts; you have no fear of Him before your eyes. Like the men of Israel, you have set up your idols *in your heart*. Your god is custom, fashion, business, pleasure, ambition, honour. You have made unto yourselves gods of these things; you have said, "These be thy gods, O Israel." Ye follow after the things which perish, the things of this world, which are vanity. O ye sons of men, think not that God is blind. He can perceive the idols in your hearts; he understandeth what be the secret things that your souls lust after; he searcheth your heart, he trieth your reins; beware lest he find you sacrificing to strange gods, for his anger will smoke against you, and his jealousy will be stirred. O ye that worship not God, the God of Israel, who give him not dominion over your whole soul, and live not to his honour, repent ye of your idolatry, seek mercy through the blood of Jesus, and provoke not the Lord to jealousy any more.

Even *believers* may be reproved on this subject. God is very jealous of his deity in the hearts of his own people. Mother, what will he say of you, if that darling child occupies a more prominent place in your love than your Lord and Saviour Jesus Christ? Husband, what shall he say to you, and with what stripes shall he smite you, when your wife reigns as a goddess in your spirit? And wife, thou shouldest love thy husband—thou doest well in so doing; but if thou exaltest him above God, if thou makest him to have dominion over thy conscience, and art willing to forsake thy Lord to please him, then thou hast made to thyself another god, and God is jealous with thee. Ay, and we may thus provoke him with the dead as well as with the living. A grief carried to excess, a grief nurtured until it prevents our attention to duty, a grief which makes us murmur and repine against the will of Providence, is sheer rebellion; it hath in it the very spirit of idolatry; it will provoke the Lord to anger, and he will surely chasten yet again, until our spirit becomes resigned to his rod. "Hast thou not forgiven God yet?" was the language of an old Quaker when he saw a widow who for years had worn her weeds, and was inconsolable in her grief—"Hast thou not forgiven God yet?" We may weep under bereavements, for Jesus wept; but we must not sorrow so as to provoke the Lord to anger, we must not act as if our friends were more precious to us than our God. We are permitted to take solace in each other, but when we carry love to idolatry, and put the creature into the Creator's place, and rebel, and fret, and bitterly repine, then the Lord hath a rod in his hand, and he will make us feel its weight, for he is a jealous God. I fear there are some professors who put their house, their garden, their business, their skill, I know not what, at seasons into the place of God. It were not consistent with the life of godliness for a man to be perpetually an idolator, but even true believers will sometimes be overcome with this sin, and will have to mourn over it. Brethren, set up no images of jealousy, but like Jacob of old cry to yourselves and to your families, "Put away the strange gods that are among you, and be clean." Let me warn those of you who neglect this that if you be the Lord's people you shall soon smart for it, and the sooner the better for your own salvation; while, on the other hand, to those ungodly persons who continue to live for objects other than divine, let me say, you not only smart in this life by bitter disappointments, but you shall also suffer eternal wrath in the life to come.

Come, let me push this matter home upon your consciences; let me carry this as at point of bayonet. Why, my hearers, there are some of you who never worship God. I know you go up to his house, but then it is only to be seen, or to quiet your conscience by having done your duty. How many of you merchants aim only to accumulate a fortune! How many of you tradesmen are living only for your families! How many young men breathe only for pleasure! How many young women exist only for amusement and vanity. I fear that some among you make your belly your god, and bow down to your own personal charms or comforts. Talk of idolators! They are here to-day! If we desire to preach to those who break the first and second commandments we have no need to go to Hindostan, or traverse the plains of Africa. They are here. Unto you who bow not before the Lord let these words be given, and let them ring in your ears—"The Lord whose name is jealous, is a jealous God." Who shall stand before him when once he is angry? When his jealousy burneth like fire and smoketh like a furnace, who shall endure the day of his wrath. Beware, lest he tear you in pieces, and there be none to deliver. Dreadful shall it be for you, if at the last you shall behold an angry God sitting in judgment. Pause now and meditate upon your doom, and think you see the Almighty robed in tempest and whirlwind.

> " His throne a seat of dreadful wrath,
> Girt with devouring flame ;
> The Lord appears consuming fire,
> And Jealous is his name."

God save you for Jesus' sake.

II. The Lord IS JEALOUS OF HIS SOVEREIGNTY.

He that made heaven and earth has a right to rule his creatures as he wills. The potter hath power over the clay to fashion it according to his own good pleasure, and the creatures being made are bound to be obedient to their Lord. He has a right to issue commands, he has done so—they are holy, and just, and wise; men are bound to obey, but, alas, they continually revolt against his sovereignty, and will not obey him; nay, there be men who deny altogether that he is King of kings, and others who take counsel together saying, " Let us break his bands in sunder, and cast away his cords from us." He that sitteth in the heavens is moved to jealousy by these sins, and will defend the rights of his crown against all comers, for the Lord is a great God, and a great King above all gods.

This reminds us of *the Lord's hatred of sin*. Every time we sin, we do as much as say, " I do not acknowledge God to be my sovereign ; I will do as I please." Each time we speak an ill-word we really say, " My tongue is my own, he is not Lord over my lips." Yea, and every-time the human heart wandereth after evil, and lusteth for that which is forbidden, it attempts to dethrone God, and to set up the Evil One in his place. The language of sin is " Who is the Lord that I should obey his voice ; I will not have God to reign over me." Sin is a deliberate treason against the majesty of God, an assault upon his crown, an insult offered to his throne. Some sins, especially, have rebellion written on their forehead—presumptuous sins, when a man's con-science has been enlightened, and he knows better, and yet still forsakes the good and follows after evil ; when a man's conscience has been aroused through some judgment, or sickness, or under a faithful ministry ; if that man returns, like a dog to his vomit, he has, indeed, insulted the sovereignty of God. But have we not all done this, and are there not some here in particular of whom we once had good hope, but who have turned back again to crooked ways? Are there not some of you who, Sabbath after Sabbath, get your consciences so quickened that you cannot be easy in sin as others are, and though you may, perhaps, indulge in sin, yet it costs you very dearly, for you know better? Did I not hear of one who sits in these seats often, but is as often on the ale bench? Did I not hear of another who can sing with us the hymns of Zion, but is equally at home with the lascivious music of the drunkard ? Do we not know of some who in their business are anything but what they should be, and yet for a show can come up to the house of God? Oh, sirs, oh, sirs, ye do provoke the Lord to jealousy! Take heed, for when he cometh out of his resting-place, and taketh to himself his sword and buckler, who are you that you should stand before the dread majesty of His presence! Tremble and be still! Humble yourselves, and repent of this your sin.

Surely, if sin attacks the sovereignty of God, *self-righteousness is equally guilty of treason:* for as sin boasts, "I will not keep God's law," self-righteousness exclaims, "I will not be saved in God's way; I will make a new road to heaven; I will not bow before God's grace; I will not accept the atonement which God has wrought out in the person of Jesus; I will be my own redeemer; I will enter heaven by my own strength, and glorify my own merits." The Lord is very wroth against self-righteousness. I do not know of anything against which his fury burneth more than against this, because this touches him in a very tender point, it insults the glory and honour of his Son Jesus Christ. Joshua said to the children of Israel when they promised to keep the law—"Ye ✳ cannot serve the Lord, for he is an holy God; he is a jealous God; and he will not forgive your transgressions nor your sins." So I may well say to every self-righteous person, "You cannot keep the law, for God is a jealous God," carefully marking every fault, and just to mark your iniquities; nor will he forgive your iniquities so long as you attempt to win his favour by works of law. Throw away thy self-righteousness, thou proud one; cast it with all other idols to the moles and to the bats, for there is no hope for thee so long as thou dost cling to it. Self-righteousness is in itself the very height and crowning-point of rebellion against God. For a man to say, "Lord, I have not sinned," is the gathering-up, the emphasis, the climax of iniquity, and God's jealousy is hot against it.

Let me add, dear friends, I feel persuaded that *false doctrine,* inasmuch as it touches God's sovereignty, is always an object of divine jealousy. Let me indicate especially the doctrines of free-will. I know there are some good men who hold and preach them, but I am persuaded that the Lord must be grieved with their doctrine though he forgives them their sin of ignorance. Free-will doctrine—what does it? It magnifies man into God; it declares God's purposes a nullity, since they cannot be carried out unless men are willing. It makes God's will a waiting servant to the will of man, and the whole covenant of grace dependant upon human action. Denying election on the ground of injustice it holds God to be a debtor to sinners, so that if he gives grace to one he is bound to do so to all. It teaches that the blood of Christ was shed equally for all men and since some are lost, this doctrine ascribes the difference to man's own will, thus making the atonement itself a powerless thing until the will of man gives it efficacy. Those sentiments dilute the scriptural description of man's depravity, and by imputing strength to fallen humanity, rob the Spirit of the glory of his effectual grace: this theory says in effect that *it is* of him that willeth, and of him that runneth, and not of God that showeth mercy. Any doctrine, my brethren, which stands in opposition to this truth—"I will have mercy on whom I will have mercy," provokes God's jealousy. I often tremble in this pulpit lest

I should utter anything which should oppose the sovereignty of my God; and though you know I am not ashamed to preach the responsibility of man to God—if God be a sovereign, man must be bound to obey him—on the other hand, I am equally bold to preach that God has a right to do what he wills with his own, that he giveth no account of his matters and none may stay his hand, or say unto him, "What doest thou?" I believe that the free-will heresy assails the sovereignty of God, and mars the glory of his dominion. In all faithfulness, mingled with sorrow, I persuade you who have been deluded by it, to see well to your ways and receive the truth which sets God on high, and lays the creature in the dust. "The Lord reigneth," be this our joy. The Lord is our King, let us obey him and defend to the death the crown rights of the King of kings, for he is a jealous God.

While tarrying upon this subject, I ought also to remark that *all the boastings of ungodly men*, whenever they exalt themselves, seeing that they are a sort of claim of sovereignty, must be very vexatious to God, the Judge of all. When you glory in your own power, you forget that power belongeth only unto God, and you provoke his jealousy. When kings, parliaments, or synods, trespass upon the sacred domains of conscience, and say to men, "Bow down, that we may go over you"—when we make attempts to lord over another man's judgment, and to make our own opinions supreme, the Lord is moved to jealousy, for he retains the court of conscience for himself alone to reign in. Let us humbly bow before the dignity of the Most High, and pay our homage at his feet.

"Glory to th' eternal King,
  Clad in majesty supreme!
Let all heaven his praises sing,
  Let all worlds his power proclaim,

O let my transported soul
  Ever on his glories gaze!
Ever yield to his control,
  Ever sound his lofty praise!"

Let us crown him every day! Let our holy obedience, let our devout lives, let our hearty acquiescence in all his will, let our reverent adoration before the greatness of his majesty, all prove that we acknowledge him to be King of kings, and Lord of lords, lest we provoke a jealous God to anger.

III. THE LORD IS JEALOUS OF HIS GLORY.

God's glory is the result of his nature and acts. He is glorious in his character, for there is such a store of everything that is holy, and good, and lovely in God, that he must be glorious. The actions which flow from his character, the deeds which are the outgoings of his inner nature, these are glorious too; and the Lord is very careful that all flesh should see that he is a good, and gracious, and just God; and he is mindful, too, that his great and mighty acts should not give glory to others, but only to himself.

How, careful, then, should we be when we do anything for God, and God is pleased to accept of our doings, that we never congratulate our-

selves. The minister of Christ should unrobe himself of every rag of praise. "You preached well," said a friend to John Bunyan one morning. "You are too late," said honest John, "the devil told me that before I left the pulpit." The devil often tells God's servants a great many things which they should be sorry to hear. Why, you can hardly be useful in a Sunday School but he will say to you—"How well you have done it!" You can scarcely resist a temptation, or set a good example, but he will be whispering to you—"What an excellent person you must be!" It is, perhaps, one of the hardest struggles of the Christian life to learn this sentence—"Not unto us, not unto us, but unto thy name be glory." Now God is so jealous on this point that, while he will forgive his own servants a thousand things, this is an offence for which he is sure to chasten us. Let a believer once say, "I am," and God will soon make him say "I am not." Let a Christian begin to boast, "I can do all things," without adding "through Christ which strengtheneth me," and before long he will have to groan, "I can do nothing," and bemoan himself in the dust. Many of the sins of true Christians, I do not doubt, have been the result of their glorifying themselves. Many a man has been permitted by God to stain a noble character and to ruin an admirable reputation, because the character and the reputation had come to be the man's own, instead of being laid, as all our crowns must be laid, at the feet of Christ. Thou mayest build the city, but if thou sayest with Nebuchadnezzar, "Behold this great Babylon which I have builded!" thou shalt be smitten to the earth. The worms which ate Herod when he gave not God the glory are ready for another meal; beware of vain glory!

How careful ought we to be *to walk humbly before the Lord.* The moment we glorify ourselves, since there is room for one glory only in the universe, we set ourselves up as rivals to the Most High. Penitent souls are always accepted, because they are not in God's way; proud souls are always rejected, because they are in God's way. Shall the insect of an hour glorify itself against the Sun which warmed it into life? Shall the potsherd exalt itself above the man that fashioned it upon the wheel? Shall the dust of the desert strive with the whirl-wind? Or the drops of the ocean struggle with the tempest? O thou nothingness and vanity, thou puny mortal called man, humble thyself and reverence thy Great Creator.

Let us see to it *that we never misrepresent God, so as to rob him of his honour.* If any minister shall preach of God so as to dishonour him, God will be jealous against that man. I fear that the Lord hath heavy wrath against those who lay the damnation of man at God's door, for they dishonour God, and he is very jealous of his name. And those, on the other hand, who ascribe salvation to man must also be heavily beneath God's displeasure, for they take from him his glory. Ah, thieves! ah, thieves! will ye dare to steal the crown-jewels of the universe! Whither go ye, whither bear ye the bright pearls which ought to shine upon the brow of Christ? To put them on the brow of man? Stop! stop! for the Lord will not give his glory to another! Give unto the Lord, all ye righteous, give unto the Lord glory and strength; give unto him the honour that is due unto his name! Any doctrine which does not give all the honour to God must provoke him to jealousy.

Be careful, dear friends, that you do not misrepresent God *yourselves*. You who murmur; you who say that God deals hardly with you, you give God an ill character; when you look so melancholy, worldlings say, "The religion of Jesus is intolerable;" and so you stain the honour of God. Oh, do not do this, for he is a jealous God, and he will surely use the rod upon you if you do.

A flash of holy pleasure crosses my mind. I am glad that he is a jealous God. It is enough to make us walk very carefully, but, at the same time, it should make us very joyful to think that the Lord is very jealous of his own honour. Then, brethren, if we believe in Christ, you and I are safe, because it would dishonour him if we were not; for his own name's sake and for his faithfulness' sake, he will never leave one of his people; since "His honour is engaged to save the meanest of his sheep." Now, if Christ could trifle with his own honour, if he had no jealousy, you and I might be afraid that he would suffer us to perish; but it never shall be. It shall be said on earth and sung in heaven at the last, that God has suffered no dishonourable defeats from the hands of either men or devils. "I chose my people," saith the Eternal Father, "and they are mine now that I make up my jewels." "I bought my people," saith the eternal Son, "I became a surety for them before the Most High, and the infernal lion could not rend the meanest of the sheep." "I quickened my people," saith the Holy Spirit; the temptations of hell could not throw them down; their own corruptions could not overpower them; I have gotten the victory in every one of them, not one of them is lost; they are all brought safely to my right hand." Hide yourselves, then, under the banner of Jehovah's jealousy. It is bloody red, I know; its ensign bears a thunderbolt and a flame of fire; but hide yourselves, hide yourselves under it, for what enemy shall reach you there? If it be to God's glory to save me, I am entrenched behind munitions of stupendous rock. If it would render God inglorious to let me, a poor sinner, descend into hell; if it would open the mouths of devils and make men say that God is not faithful to his promise, then am I secure, for God's glory is wrapped up with my salvation, and the one cannot fail because the other cannot be tarnished. Beloved, let us mind that we be very jealous of God's glory ourselves since he is jealous of it. Let us say with Elijah—"I am very jealous for the Lord God of hosts." May our lives, and conduct, and conversation prove that we are jealous of our hearts lest they should once depart from him; and may we smite with stern and unrelenting hand every sin and every thought of pride that might touch the glory of our gracious God; living to him as living before a jealous God.

IV. In the highest sense, THE LORD IS JEALOUS OVER HIS OWN PEOPLE.

Let me only hint, that human jealousy, although it will exercise itself over man's reputation, rights, and honour, hath one particularly tender place: jealousy guardeth, like an armed man, *the marriage-covenant*. A suspicion here is horrible. Even good old Jacob, when he came to die, could not look upon his son Reuben without remembering his offence. " He went up to my couch," said the old man—and, as if the remembrance was too painful for him, he hurried on from Reuben to the next. The Lord has been graciously pleased to say of his people, " I am married unto you." The covenant of grace is a marriage-covenant, and Christ's Church has become his spouse. It is here that God's jealousy is peculiarly liable to take fire. Men cannot be God's favourites without being the subjects of his watchfulness and jealousy: that which might be looked over in another, will be chastened in a member of Christ. As a husband is jealous of his honour, so is the Lord Jesus much concerned for the purity of his Church.

The Lord Jesus Christ, of whom I now speak, *is very jealous of your love*, O believer. Did he not choose you? He cannot bear that you should choose another. Did he not buy you with his own blood? He cannot endure that you should think you are your own, or that you belong to this world. He loved you with such a love that he could not stop in heaven without you ; he would sooner die than that you should perish; he stripped himself to nakedness that he might clothe you with beauty ; he bowed his face to shame and spitting that he might lift you up to honour and glory, and he cannot endure that you should love the world, and the things of the world. His love is strong as death towards you, and therefore will be cruel as the grave. He will be as a cruel one towards you if you do not love him with a perfect heart. He will take away that husband ; he will smite that child; he will bring you from riches to poverty, from health to sickness, even to the gates of the grave, because he loves you so much that he cannot endure that anything should stand between your heart's **love** and him. Be careful Christians, you that are married to Christ ; remember, you are married to a jealous husband.

He is very jealous *of your trust*. He will not permit you to trust in an arm of flesh. He will not endure that you should hew out broken cisterns, when the overflowing fountain is always free to you. When we come up from the wilderness leaning upon our Beloved, then is our Beloved glad, but when we go down to the wilderness leaning on some other arm ; when we trust in our own wisdom or the wisdom of a friend —worst of all, when we trust in any works of our own, he is angry, and will smite us with heavy blows that he may bring us to himself.

He is also very jealous *of our company*. It were well if a Christian could see nothing but Christ. When the wife of a Persian noble had been invited to the coronation of Darius, the question was asked of her by her husband—"Did you not think the king a most beautiful man?" and her answer was--"I cared not to look at the king; my eyes are for my husband only, for my heart is his." The Christian should say the same. There is nothing beneath the spacious **arch** of heaven comparable to Christ: there should be no one with whom we converse so much as with Jesus. To abide in him only, this is true love ; but to commune with the world, to find solace in our comforts, to be loving this evil world, this is vexing to our jealous Lord. Do you not believe that nine out of ten of the troubles and pains of believers are the result of their love to some other person than Christ? Nail me to thy cross, thou bleeding Saviour! Put thy thorn-crown upon my head to be a hedge to keep my thoughts within its bound! O for a fire to burn up all my wandering loves. O for a seal to stamp the name of my Beloved indelibly upon my heart! O love divine expel from me all carnal worldly loves, and fill me with thyself!

Dear friends, let this jealousy which should keep us near to Christ *be also a comfort* to us, for if we be married to Christ, and he be jealous of us, depend upon it this jealous husband will let none touch his spouse. Joel tells us that the Lord is jealous for his land, and Zechariah utters the word of the Lord, "I am jealous for Jerusalem, and for Zion with a great jealousy;" and then he declares that he will punish the heathen. And will he not avenge his own elect who cry unto him day and night? There is not a hard word spoken but the Lord shall avenge it! There is not a single deed done against us, but the strong hand of him who once died but now lives for us, shall take terrible vengeance upon all his adversaries. I am not afraid for the Church of God! I tremble not for the cause of God! Our jealous Husband will never let his Church be in danger, and if any smite her he will give them double for every blow. The gates of hell shall not prevail against his Church, but she shall prevail against the gates of hell. Her jealous Husband shall roll away her shame; her reproach shall be forgotten; her glory shall be fair as the moon, clear as the sun, and terrible as an army with banners, for he that is jealous of himself is jealous for her fair fame. The subject is large and deep; let us prove that we understand it, by henceforth walking very carefully; and if any say "Why are you so precise?" let this be our answer—"I serve a jealous God."

The Root of the Matter

"The root of the matter is found in me."—Job xix. 28.

FOR the last three or four Lord's-day evenings I have been trying to fish with a net of small meshes. It has been my anxious desire to gather in, and draw to shore the Much-Afraids, the Fearings, the Despondencies, and those of Little-Faith who seem to think it scarcely possible that they could belong to the people of God at all. I hope those sermons which have taken the lowest evidences of Christian life, and have been adapted rather to babes in grace than to those who are strong men in our Israel, will furnish comfort to many who beforetime had been bowed down with distress.

In pursuance of the same purpose this evening, I take up the expressive figure of our text to address myself to those who evidently have the grace of God embedded in their hearts, though they put forth little blossom and bear little fruit; that they may be consoled, if so be there is clear evidence that at least the root of the matter is found in them. Incidentally, however, the same truth may be profitable, not only to the saplings in the garden of the Lord, but to the most goodly trees; for there are times and seasons when their branches do not put out much luxuriant foliage, and the hidden life furnishes the only true argument of their vitality.

I. Our first aim then will be TO SPEAK OF THOSE THINGS WHICH ARE ESSENTIAL TO TRUE GODLINESS IN CONTRAST, OR, I might better say, IN COMPARISON WITH OTHER THINGS WHICH ARE TO BE REGARDED AS SHOOTS RATHER THAN AS ROOT AND GROUNDWORK.

The tree can do without some of its branches, though the loss of them might be an injury; but it cannot live at all without its roots: the roots are essential; take those away, and the plant must wither. And thus my dear friends, there are things essential in the Christian religion. There are essential *doctrines*, essential *experiences*, and there is essential *practice*.

With regard to essential *doctrines*. It is very desirable for us to be established in the faith. A very happy thing it is to have been taught from one's youth up the sound and solid doctrines which comforted the

Puritans, which made blessed the heart of Luther and of Calvin, fired the zeal of Chrysostom and Augustine, and flashed like lightning from the lips of Paul. By such judicious training we are no doubt delivered from many doubts and difficulties which an evil system of theology would be sure to encourage. The man who is sound in the faith, and who understands the higher and sublimer doctrines of divine revelation, will have wells of consolation which the less instructed cannot know. But we always believe, and are ever ready to confess, that there are many doctrines which, though exceedingly precious, are not so essential but that a person may be in a state of grace and yet not receive them. For instance—God forbid that we should regard a belief in the doctrine of *election* as an absolute test of a man's salvation, for no doubt there are many precious sons of God who have not been able to receive that precious truth ; of course the doctrine is essential to the great scheme of grace, as the foundation of God's eternal purpose, but it is not, therefore, necessarily the root of faith in the sinner's reception of the gospel. And, perhaps, too, I may put down the doctrine of *the final perseverance of the saints* in the same list. There be many who. no doubt, will persevere to the end, but who yet cannot accept the possibility of being assured thereof ; they are so occupied with the thoughts of their probation that they come not to the mature knowledge of their full salvation. They are securely kept while they credit not their security, just as there are thousands of the elect who cannot believe in election. Though Calvinistic doctrine is so dear to us, we feel ready to die in its defence, yet we would by no means set it up as being a test of a man's spiritual state. We wish all our brethren saw with us, but a man may be almost blind, and yet he may live. A man with weak eye-sight and imperfect vision may be able to enter into the kingdom of heaven ; indeed, it is better to enter there having but one eye, than, having two eyes and being orthodox in doctrine, to be cast into hell fire. But there are some distinct truths of revelation that are essential in such sense, that those who have not accepted them cannot be called Christians, and those who wilfully reject them are exposed to the fearful anathemas which are hurled against apostacy. I shall not go into a detailed list. Let it suffice, that I give you a few striking illustrations. *The doctrine of the Trinity we must ever look upon as being one of the roots of the matter.* When men go unsound here, we suspect that, ere long, they will be wrong everywhere. The moment you get any suspicion of a man's wavering about the Divinity of Christ, you have not long to wait before you discover that on all other points he has gone wrong. Well did John Newton express it—

> " What think you of Christ is the test
> To try both your state, and your scheme ;
> You cannot be right in the rest,
> Unless you think rightly of him."

Almost all the forms of error that have sprung up since the days of Dr. Doddridge, when sundry gentlemen began to talk against the proper Deity of the Son of God—all the forms of error, I say, whatever department of the Christian system they may have been supposed to attack,—

have really stabbed at the Deity of our Redeemer. That is the one thing that they are angry at, as if their mother-wit taught them it was the true line of demarcation between natural and revealed religion. They cannot bear that the glorious Lord should be unto us a place of broad rivers and streams, and so they try to do without him; but their tacklings are loosed, they cannot well strengthen their mast, they cannot spread the sail. A gospel without belief in the living and true God— Trinity in Unity, and Unity in Trinity—is a rope of sand. As well hope to make a pyramid stand upon its apex as to make a substantial gospel when the real and personal Deity of the Father, the Son, and the Holy Ghost is left as a moot or disputed point. But I ought to mention the strange incoherency of that discourse, which sets forth the influences of the Spirit without a due regard to his Personal Agency. Oh! how little is the Holy Spirit known! We get beyond the mere exercise of opinions, when we believe in Christ, know the Father, and receive the Holy Ghost. This is to have a knowledge of the true God and eternal life. Likewise essential is the doctrine of *the vicarious sacrifice of our Lord Jesus Christ.* Any bell that does not ring sound on that point had better be melted down directly. I do not think we have many in our denomination—we have some who are not very clear—still I think we have but few that are unsound in the doctrine of the real substitution of Christ. But there are plenty elsewhere; perhaps I need not indicate the locality, for in the denomination where they seem to be tolerably prolific they have one earnest tongue and one ready pen that is always willing at all times to expose the miscreants who thus do damage to the cause of Christ, by giving up the precious blood of Jesus as the sole cause of the remission of sins and the only means of access to God. Why, my brethren, we have nothing else left after we have given up this choice seal of the everlasting covenant, on which all our hopes depend. Renounce the doctrine of Jesus dying in our place, room, and stead! Better for us all to be offered as one great heca- tomb, one mighty sacrifice to God on one fire, than to tolerate for a moment any doubts about that which is the world's hope, heaven's joy, hell's terror, and eternity's song. I marvel how men are permitted to stand in the pulpit and preach at all who dare to say anything against the atonement of Christ. I find in the Dutch Church, in the French Church, and in the German Churches, that men are accepted as Christian ministers who will yet speak hard things against the atonement itself, and even against the Deity of Him by whom the atonement was made. There is no other religion in the world that has been false to its own doctrines in the way that Christianity has been. Imagine a Mahometan allowed to come forward in the pulpit and preach against Mahomet! Would it be tolerated for a single moment? Suppose a Brahmin fed and paid to stand up in a temple and speak against Brahma! Would it be allowed? No surely; nor is there an infidel lecturer in this country but would find his pay stopped at once, if, while pretending to be in the service of Atheism, he declaimed the sentiments he was deputed to advocate. How is it? Why is it? In the name of everything that is reasonable and instinc- tively consistent, whence can it be, that men can be called Christian ministers after the last vestige of Christianity has been treacherously repudiated by them? How is it that they can be tolerated to minister in holy things to people who profess and call themselves sincere followers of Jesus, when they tread under foot the precious blood of Christ, "reduce the mystery of godliness to a system of ethics;" (to use the words of a divine of the last century) " degrade the Christian Church into a school of philosophy; deny the expiation made by our Redeemer's sacrifice; obscure the brightest manifestation of divine mercy; undermine the principal pillar of practical religion; and to make a desperate shipwreck of *our* everlasting interests, they dash *themselves* to death on the very rock of salvation." No; we must have the atonement, and that not tacitly acknowledged, but openly set forth. Charity can go a good way, but charity cannot remove the altar from the door of the Tabernacle, or admit the worshipper into the most Holy Place without the blood of propitiation. So, again, the doctrine of *justification by faith* is one of the roots of the matter. You know Luther's saying; I need not repeat it; it is the article of a standing or falling Church, " By grace are ye saved through faith, and that not of yourselves, it is the gift of God ; not of works lest any man should boast." Do you preach that doctrine? My hand and my heart are stretched out to you! Do you deny it? Do you stutter over it? Are you half-afraid of it? My back must be turned against you; I know nothing of you; you are none of the Lord's! What saith the Apostle Paul to you? Would he have communed with you? He lifts his hand to heaven and he says—" If any man preach any other gospel than that ye have received let him be accursed!" That is Paul's saintly greeting ; that is Paul's Apostolic malediction—an " Anathema Maranatha" upon the man that preaches not the Lord Jesus, and who does not vindicate the great doctrine of salvation by grace and not by works. Well now, friend, you may have come in here to listen to our doctrine, and to judge whether you can hold fellowship with us. We have been talking about the root of the matter. Permit me to say that if you are sound on these three points, the One God in Trinity, the glorious doctrine of the substitution of Christ in the place of sinners, and the plan of salvation by simple faith in Jesus, then inasmuch as these roots of the matter are in you, God forbid that we should exclude you as heretical. If you are in other points unenlightened, and groping about in uncertainty, doubtless the Lord will teach you, but we believe the root of the matter is in you so far as doctrine is concerned.

Turning to another department of my subject; *there are certain root-matters in reference to experience.* It is a very happy thing to have a deep experience of *one's own depravity.* It may seem strange, but so it is, a man will scarcely ever have high views of the preciousness of the Saviour who has not also had deep views of the evil of his own heart. High houses, you know, need deep foundations; and when God digs deep and throws out the mire of self-sufficiency, then he puts in the great stone of Christ's all-sufficiency, and builds us up high in union and fellowship with him. To read the guilt of sin in the lurid glare of Mount Sinai, to hear the thunderings, and shrink back in wild dismay at the utter hopelessness of approach to God by the law, is a most profitable lesson. Ay, and to see the guilt of sin in the mellow light of Mount Calvary, and to feel that contrition, which a view of Christ crucified alone can produce—this is to prepare the heart for such an ecstacy of joy in God, through whom we have now received the atonement, as surpasses, I verily believe, the common experience of Christians. Still I dare not make a criterion of the profound depths of anguish with which some of us have had the sentence of death in ourselves. But it is absolutely essential that you should be brought to the end of all perfection in the flesh—that all your hopes of legal righteousness should expire—that you should be dead to the law, in order that you may live unto God. This death may be with painful struggles, or it may be tranquil as a sleep; you may be smitten suddenly, as though an arrow from the Almighty were transfixed in your heart; or you may pine away by a slow and tedious consumption. Yet die you must, before you can be made partaker of resurrection. This much, however, I will venture to say, you may be really a child of God, and yet the plague of your own heart may be but very little understood. You must know something of it, for no man ever did or ever will come to Christ unless he has first learned to loathe himself, and to see that in him, that is in his flesh, there dwelleth no good thing. You may not be able to talk, as some do, of conflicts within, and of the fountain of the great deep of your natural sin, and yet you may be, for all that, a true child of God. It is a happy thing, too, to have an experience which *keeps close to Christ Jesus;* to know what the word "communion" means, without needing to take down another man's biography; to understand Solomon's Song without a commentary; to read it through and through, and say "Precious Book! thou didst express just what I have felt, but what I never could have expressed." But, dear friends, though all this be well, remember it is not essential. It is not a sign that you are not converted because you cannot understand what it is to sit under his shadow with great delight. You may have been converted, and yet hardly have come so far as that. Always distinguish between the branches of the matter and the root of the matter. It is well to have branches like the cedars, and to send up your shoots towards heaven, but it is the root that is the all-important thing—the root of the matter. Now what is the root of the matter experimentally? Well, I think the real root of it is what Job has been talking about in the verses preceding the text—"I know," saith he, "that my Redeemer liveth." We talked of that this morning. The root of the matter in Christian experience is to know that Jesus Christ, the Son of God, is able to save to the uttermost all them that come unto God by him, and to know this by a personal appropriation of his power to save *by a simple act of faith.* In fine, dear friend, thou hast the root of the matter in thee if thy soul can say—

> "My hope is built on nothing less
> Than Jesus' blood and righteousness;
> I dare not trust the sweetest frame,
> But wholly lean on Jesus' name:
> On Christ the solid rock I stand,
> All other ground is sinking sand."

There must be in connection with this the *repentance of sin*, but this repentance may be far from perfect, and thy faith in Christ may be far from strong; but, oh! if thou hatest sin, if thou desirest to be rid of it, if it be thy plague, thy burden, thy grief; if Christ Jesus be thine only comfort, thy help, thy hope, thy trust, then understand, this is the root of the matter. I wish there were more than the root, but inasmuch as that is there, it is enough—thou art accepted before God, for the root of the matter is in thee. A living faith in a living Saviour, and a real death to all creature-merit and to all hope in creature-strength; this I take it is that which is the root of the matter in spiritual experience.

Did I not say that there was a root of the matter *practically?* Yes, and I would to God that we all practically had the branches and the fruits. These will come in their season, and they must come, if we are Christ's disciples; but nobody expects to see fruit on a tree a week after it has been planted. You know there are some trees that do not bring forth any great fruit till they have been in the ground some two or three years, and then at last, when the favourable season comes, they are white with blossoms, and by-and-bye are bowed to the earth with luscious fruit. It is very desirable that all Christians should be full of zeal, should be vehemently earnest, should go about doing good, should minister to the poor, should teach the ignorant, and comfort the distressed, yet these things cannot be called the real root of the matter. The real root of the matter practically is this—" One thing I know; whereas I was blind now I see; the things I once loved I now hate; the things I once hated I love; now it is no more the world, but God; no more the flesh, but Christ; no more pleasure, but obedience; no more what I will, but what Jesus wills." If any of you can from your souls say that you desire the tenour of your life to be, " Lord, not as I will, but as thou wilt," you have got the root of the matter practically.

Let me guard this part of my subject with one further remark. There are those who do certain duties with a conscientious motive, in order to make themselves Christians—such as observing the Sabbath, holding daily worship of God in their families, and attending the public services of the Lord's house with regularity. But they do not distinguish between these external acts—which may be but the ornaments that clothe a graceless life, and those fruits of good living that grow out of a holy constitution, which is the root of genuine obedience. Some habits and practises of godly men may be easily counterfeited. Yet I think that there are certain virtues of God's children which are perfectly inimitable. " To bear reproach for Christ, and to suffer wrong patiently," is, to my mind very much like the root in practical godliness. Perhaps there is a timid girl now present who has braved for many a month the persecution of her father and mother, to serve that Saviour whom her parents never knew. Nobody knows what rough words and hard treatment she has had to encounter—all because she will come to chapel, and she will steal away into her own room sometimes, and she always has the bible in her hand when she goes in, and she generally looks as if she had been crying when she comes out. Ah, poor soul! I doubt not the root of the matter is in thee. Or, see there a young man who has risked losing his situation, because he will not conceal his attachment to Christ. Such as these are sometimes brought into great straits. They do not see any precept that plainly says "Thou shalt do this," or "Thou shalt not do that." But they find they must be one thing or the other. They make their choice, and it is against their worldly interests, but it is done for the love they bear to a Saviour's name. Their gentle courage I admire. Their little faith takes a strong grip. Oh! I cannot doubt the root of the matter is found in them. There is practical evidence of it.

Let me pause here for a moment before leaving this first point to notice that you may generally ascertain whether you have got the root of the matter by its characteristic properties. You know a root is *a fixing thing.* Plants without roots may be thrown over the wall; they may be passed from hand to hand; but a root is a fixed thing. How firmly the oaks are rooted in the ground! You may think of those old oaks in the park; ever so far off you have seen the roots coming out of the ground, and then they go in again, and you have said, "Why! what do these thick fibres belong to?" Surely they belong to one of those old oaks ever so far away. They had sent that root there to get a good holdfast, so that when the March wind comes through the forest, and other trees are torn up—fir trees, perhaps; trees that have outgrown their strength at the top, while they have too little hold at bottom,—the old oaks bow to the tempest, curtsey to the storm, and anon they lift up their branches again in calm dignity; they cannot be blown down. Well now; if you have got the root of the matter you are fixed; you are fixed to God, fixed to Christ, fixed to things divine. If you are tempted, you are not soon carried away. Oh! how many professors there are that have no roots! Get them into godly company, and they are such saints; but get them with other company, and what if I say that they are devils! There you have them. Their mother is come up from the country, and she asked them to come to-night to hear Spurgeon. Here they are. Mother will not know but what John is one of the best lads anywhere while she is in town. Ah! but if it happens to be uncle William that comes up to London in a month's time, and he should ask them to go to a theatre! O yes, they will go there too, and he will never know that they have any religion, for they will put that by until he is gone again. They have no roots. Give me the man that is bound hard and fast to Christ; lashed to the cross by cords that even the knives of hell cannot sever; lashed to the cross for ever! You have no roots unless you can say, "O God! my heart is fixed, my heart is fixed; by stern resolve and by firm covenant thine I am; bind the sacrifice with cords, even unto the horns of the altar."

Again, a root is not only a fixing thing, but a *quickening thing.* What is it that first sets the sap a flowing in the spring? Why, it is the root. Down below beneath the earth it begins to feel the genial influence of the coming spring, and it talks to the trunk and says, "It is time to set the sap flowing;" so the sap begins to flow, and the buds begin to burst. Ah! and you must have a vital principle; you must have a living principle. Some Christians are like those toys they import from France, which have sand in them; the sand runs down, and some little invention turns and works them as long as the sand is running, but when the sand is all out it stops. So on Sunday morning these people are just turned right, and the sand runs, and they work all the Sunday; but the sand runs down by Sunday night, and then they stand still, or else go on with the world's work just as they did before. Oh! this will never do! There must be a living principle; something that shall be a mainspring within; a wheel that cannot help running on, and that does not depend upon external resources.

A root, too, is *a receiving thing*. The botanists tell us a great many things about the ends of the roots, which can penetrate into the soil hunting after the particular food upon which the tree is fed. Ah! and if you have got the root of the matter in you, when you come to hear a sermon you will be sending out your root to look after the particular food which your soul wants. You will send those roots into the pages of Scripture, sometimes into a hymn book; often into the sermon; into a brother's experience, and into God's Providence, seeking that something upon which your soul can feed.

Hence it follows that the root becomes *a supplying thing*, because it is a receiving thing. We must have a religion that lives upon God, and that supplies us with strength to live for God. Oh! how divinely blessed are those men in whom the root of the matter is found!

II. Let me briefly notice in the second place that WHEREVER THERE IS THE ROOT OF THE MATTER THERE IS VERY MUCH GROUND FOR COMFORT.

Sounds there in my ears the sigh, the groan, the sad complaint?—"I do not grow as I could wish; I am not so holy as I want to be; I cannot praise and bless the Lord as I could desire; I am afraid I am not a fruitful bough whose branches run over the wall?" Yes, but is the root of the matter in you? If so, cheer up, you have cause for gratitude. Remember *that in some things you are equal to the greatest and most full-grown Christian.* You are as much bought with blood, O little saints, as are the holy brotherhood. He that bought the sheep bought the lambs too. You are as much an adopted child of God as any other Christian. A babe of a span long is as true a child of its parents as is the full-grown man. You are as truly justified, for your justification is not a thing of degrees. Your little faith has made you clean every whit; it could have done no more had it been the strongest faith in the world. You have as much right to the precious things of the covenant as the most advanced believers, for your right to covenant mercies lies not in your growth, but in the covenant itself; and your faith in Jesus may not assay to measure the extent of your inheritance in him. So then you are as rich as the richest, if not in enjoyment, yet in real possession. You are as dear to your Father's heart as the greatest among them. If there be a weakling in a family the father often loves it the most, or at least indulges it with the most caresses; and when there is a child that has lost one of its senses, be it sight or hearing, you will notice with what assiduous care the parents watch over that one. You are possibly such a tender one, but Christ is very tender over you. You are like the smoking flax; anybody else would say—"Put out that smoking flax; what a smell! How it fills the room with a foul and offensive odour!" But the smoking flax He will not quench. You are just like a bruised reed; there used to be some music in you, but now the reed is broken, and there is no tuneful note at all to be brought out from the poor, bruised, crooked, and broken reed. Any one else but the Chief Musician would pull you out and throw you away. You might think he would be sure to say—"I do not want a bruised reed; it is of no use at all among the pipes." But he will not break the bruised reed, nor quench the smoking flax. Instead of being down-cast by reason of what you are, you should begin to triumph in Christ. Am I but little in Israel? Yet in Christ I am made to sit in heavenly places. Am I poor in faith? Still in Christ I am heir of all things. Do I sometimes wander? Yet Jesus Christ comes after me and brings me back. Though "less than nothing I can boast, and vanity confess," yet, if the root of the matter be in me I will rejoice in the Lord, and glory in the God of my salvation.

III. This brings me to the third and closing part—WHEREVER THE ROOT OF THE MATTER IS, THERE WE SHOULD TAKE CARE THAT WE WATCH IT WITH TENDERNESS AND WITH LOVE.

Some of you may have the notion that you are advanced in knowledge, that you have much skill in interpreting the word of God, and that you understand the mysteries of the kingdom of heaven. It is highly possible that your notion is correct. Well! You go out into the world, and you meet with people who do not know quite so much as you do, and who have not yet learned all the doctrines of grace, as they are threaded together in the divine plan of salvation. May I persuade you not to get into controversy, not to be continually fighting and quarelling with people who do not hold just your sentiments. If you discover the root of the matter in any man, say at once—"Why should I persecute you? Why should we fall to quarrelling with each other, seeing that the root of the matter is in us both?" Save your swords for Christ's real enemies. The way to make men learn the truth is not to abuse them. We shall never make a brother see a doctrine by smiting him in the eye. Hold your lantern up and let him see. I recollect when in my boyhood I sometimes held a candle to a man who was working at night, sawing; he used to say to me—" Now, my lad, hold the candle so that you can see yourself, and you may depend upon it that I can see too." And I have generally found, that if you hold up the doctrines in such a way that you can see them yourselves, and just tell to others the way in which you have been led to see them, and how you see them now, you will often give a light to other men, if they have the root of the matter in them. Quarrel not; fight not with them, but be friends, and especially this, shew thyself friendly.

Then, again, if you meet with young professors who have the root of the matter in them, do not begin condemning them for lack of knowledge. I have heard of some old believers, ay, and of some not very old too, who had read a great deal, and had, perhaps, more in the head than in the heart; and when young enquirers came to see them, they began to ask them—" Which theory do you hold, sub-lapsarian or supra-lapsarian ?" I do not mean that they exactly said those very words, but they suggested some knotty points something of that sort; and the young people have said—" I am sure I do not know, sir." It has sometimes been the case that these young enquirers have been dealt very harshly with, and I remember one case where a certain brother—a good man too, in his way, said—" Well, now, I am sorry to tell you that you are no child of God; if you die as you are you will be lost "—only because the poor soul did not exactly know the difference between two things that are amazingly alike after all. I do not think we ought to do this. It is not policy for us to go about killing all the lambs; for if we do this, where will the sheep come from ? If we are always condemning those who have only begun as yet to learn their letters, we shall never have any readers. People must begin to say " Twice two are four, " before they can ever come to be very learned in mathematics. Should we stop them at once, and say— " You are no child of God, because you do not know how to compute the logarithms of grace? " Why, then at once we have put out of the synagogue those who might have been its best ornaments. Remember, my dear friends, that wherever we see the root of the matter, Christ has accepted the person, and therefore we ought to accept him. This is why I love to think that when we break bread at this table we always receive amongst us, as far as we know, all those who have got the root of the matter in them. I have heard a story of the late good Dr. Stedman, when he was tutor of Bradford College. It appears he was a very strict communion Baptist, and carried it out conscientiously. One day he preached for some Independents, and in the afternoon, after the service, there was to be the communion. Now Mr. Stedman prayed most earnestly that the Lord would be pleased graciously to vouchsafe his presence to the dear brethren when they met around his table. After the service was over he was going to the vestry to put on his great-coat, intending to go home. One of the deacons said—"Doctor, you will stop with us, will you not, to the communion?" "Well, my dear brother," he said—"it is no want of love, but, you see, it would compromise my principles; I am a strict communion Baptist, and I could not well stop and commune with you who have not been baptized; do not think it is any want of love now, but it is only out of respect to my principles." "Oh!" said the deacon, "but it is not your principles, because what did you pray for, Doctor? You prayed your Master, the Lord Jesus, to come to our table; and if acccording to your principles it is wrong for you to go there, you should not ask your Master to come where you must not go yourself; but if you believe that your Lord and Master will come to the table, surely where the Master is, it cannot be wrong for the servant to be." The deacon's reasoning appears to me very sound. And it is in the same spirit I say of any or to any whose sincere faith I have no reason to doubt—if they have got the root of the matter in them, "Come and welcome?" We are sorry that when our friends ought to keep the feast of tabernacles with great branches of trees they only pull small twigs, and so do not get the benefit of the broader shadow. We are sorry that when Christ tells them to be immersed they go and sprinkle, but that is their own business and not ours. To their own Master they must stand or fall, but if the root of the matter be there, why persecute ye them, seeing that the root of the matter is found in them. Let them come. God has received them, and let us do the same.

That matter about encouraging young believers, and not putting stumbling blocks in their path, may seem to some of you decidedly unimportant; but I am persuaded that there are many young Christians who have been made to suffer for years through the roughness of some more advanced believers. Christian! thou that art strong, be thou very tender towards the weak, for the day may come when thou wilt be weaker than he. Never did bullock push with side and shoulder the lean cattle of the herd when they came to drink, but what the Lord took away the glory from the fat bull of Bashan, and made him willing to associate with the very least of the herd. You cannot hector it over a child of God without making his Father angry; and though you be a child of God yourself, yet if you deal harshly with one of your brethren you shall smart for it, for the Master's rod is always ready even for his own beloved children when they are not tender with the sons and daughters of Zion, who are kept as the apple of God's eye. Remember, too, brethren, that the day may come when you will want consolation from the very friend whom you have treated so roughly. I have known some great people—some very great people, that have at last been made to sit at the feet of those whom before they called all sorts of ill names. God has his ways of taking the wind out of men's sails. While their sails were full, and the wind blew, they said, "No, no; we do not care about that little port over yonder; we do not care to put in there; it is only a miserable little fishing-village." But when the wind came howling on, and the deep rolled heavily, and it seemed as if the dread artillery of God were all mustering for the battle; ah! how with the reef-sail they have tried to fly, as best they could, into the little harbour! Do not speak ill of the little harbour. Do not be ashamed of little Christians. Stand up for the weaklings of the flock, and be this your motto, you strong Christians—

> "There's not a lamb amidst thy flock
> I would disdain to feed;
> There's not a foe before whose face
> I'd fear thy cause to plead."

Now I ask you, by way of solemn searching investigation, have you the root of the matter in you? I have spoken for your encouragement, in case you have the root of the matter in you. If you have not, there awaits you nothing but destruction, only that you are not lost hopelessly; the root of the matter is still to be had. The Holy Ghost can yet give you a new heart and a right spirit. Jesus Christ is still able and willing to save. Oh, look there! I see his five wounds; they flow with rivers of blood! Look there, sinner! and as thou lookest thou shalt live. Whoever thou mayest be, though thou art the worst sinner out of hell, yet

> "While the lamp holds out to burn,
> The vilest sinner may return."

Look there, sinner, look, look and live! I think I have closed my sermon each night lately with those words, and I will do so again to-night. There is life in a look at a crucified Saviour. There is life at this moment for thee. Oh! look to him, and thou shalt find that life for thyself. God bless you, for Jesu's sake.

May the grace of our Lord Jesus Christ, and the love of God our Father, and the fellowship of the Holy Spirit, be with all who love Jesus. now and eternally. Amen.

The Importunate Widow

" And he spake a parable unto them to this end, that men ought always to pray, and not to faint; saying, There was in a city a judge, which feared not God, neither regarded man: and there was a widow in that city; and she came unto him, saying, Avenge me of mine adversary. And he would not for a while: but afterward he said within himself, Though I fear not God, nor regard man; yet because this widow troubleth me, I will avenge her, lest by her continual coming she weary me. And the Lord said, Hear what the unjust judge saith. And shall not God avenge his own elect, which cry day and night unto him, though he bear long with them? I tell you that he will avenge them speedily."—Luke xviii. 1—8.

REMEMBER that our Lord did not only inculcate prayer with great earnestness, but he was himself a brilliant example of it. It always gives force to a teacher's words when his hearers well know that he carries out his own instructions. Jesus was a prophet mighty both in deed and in word, and we read of him, "Jesus began both to do and to teach." In the exercise of prayer, "cold mountains and the midnight air" witnessed that he was as great a doer as a teacher. When he exhorted his disciples to continue in prayer, and to " pray without ceasing," he only bade them follow in his steps. If any one of all the members of the mystical body might have been supposed to need no prayer, it would certainly have been our Covenant Head, but if our Head abounded in supplication, much more ought we, the inferior members. He was never defiled with the sins which have debased and weakened us spiritually; he had no inbred lusts to struggle with. But if the perfectly pure drew near so often unto God, how much more incessant in supplication ought we to be ! So mighty, so great, and yet so prayerful ! O ye weak ones of the flock, how forcibly does the lesson come home to you ! Imagine, therefore, the discourse of this morning is not preached to you by me, but comes fresh from the lips of one who was the great master of secret prayer, the highest paragon and pattern of private supplication, and let every word have the force about it as coming from such a One.

Turn we at once to our text, and in it we shall notice, first, *the and design of the parable;* secondly, we shall have some words to say upon *the two actors in it,* whose characters are intentionally so described as to give force to the reasoning; and then, thirdly, we shall dwell upon *the power which in the parable is represented as triumphant.*

I. First, then, consider OUR LORD'S DESIGN IN THIS PARABLE—" Men ought always to pray, and not to faint."

But can men pray always? There was a sect in the earlier days of Christianity who were foolish enough to read the passage literally, and to attempt praying without ceasing by continual repetition of prayers. They of course separated themselves from all worldly concerns, and in order to fulfil one duty of life neglected every other. Such madmen might well expect to reap the due reward of their follies. Happily there is no need in this age for us to reprobate such an error; there is far more necessity to cry out against those who, under the pretence of praying always, have no settled time for prayer at all, and so run to the opposite extreme. Our Lord meant by saying men ought always to pray, that *they ought to be always in the spirit of prayer,* always ready to pray. Like the old knights, always in warfare, not always on their steeds dashing forward with their lances in rest to unhorse an adversary, but always wearing their weapons where they could readily reach them, and always ready to encounter wounds or death for the sake of the cause which they championed. Those grim warriors often slept in their armour; so even when we sleep, we are still to be in the spirit of prayer, so that if perchance we wake in the night we may still be with God. Our soul, having received the divine centripetal influence which makes it seek its heavenly centre, should be evermore naturally rising towards God himself. Our heart is to be like those beacons and watch-towers which were prepared along the coast of England when the invasion of the Armada was hourly expected, not always blazing, but with the wood always dry, and the match always there, the whole pile being ready to blaze up at the appointed moment. Our souls should be in such a condition that ejaculatory prayer should be very frequent with us. No need to pause in business and leave the counter, and fall down upon the knees; the spirit should send up its silent, short, swift petitions to the throne of grace. When Nehemiah would ask a favour of the king, you will remember that he found an opportunity to do so through the king's asking him, " Why art thou sad ?" but before he made him an answer he says, " I prayed unto the King of heaven ;" instinctively perceiving the occasion, he did not leap forward to embrace it, but he halted just a moment to ask that he might be enabled to embrace it wisely and fulfil his great design therein. So you and I should often feel, " I cannot do this till I have asked a blessing on it." However impulsively I may spring forward to gain an advantage, yet my spirit, under the influence of divine grace, should hesitate until it has said, "If thy Spirit go not with me, carry me not up hence." A Christian should carry the weapon of all-prayer like a drawn sword in his hand. We should never sheathe our supplications. Never may our hearts be like an unlimbered gun, with everything to be done to it before it can thunder on the foe, but it should be like a piece of cannon, loaded and primed, only requiring the fire that it may be discharged. The soul should be not always in the exercise of prayer, but always in the energy of prayer ; not always actually praying, but always intentionally praying.

Further, when our Lord says, men ought always to pray, he may also have meant that *the whole life of the Christian should be a life of devotion to God.*

> " Prayer and praise, with sins forgiven,
> Bring down to earth the bliss of heaven."

To praise God for mercies received both with our voices and with our actions, and then to pray to God for the mercies that we need, devoutly acknowledging that they come from him, these two exercises in one form or other should make up the sum total of human life. Our life psalm should be composed of alternating verses of praying and of praising until we get into the next world, where the prayer may cease, and praise may swallow up the whole of our immortality. " But," saith one, " we have our daily business to attend to." I know you have, but there is a way of making business a part of praise and prayer. You say, "Give us this day our daily bread," and that is a prayer as you utter it; you go off to your work, and as you toil, if you do so in a devout spirit, you are actively praying the same prayer by your lawful labour. You praise God for the mercies received in your morning hymn ; and when you go into the duties of life, and there exhibit those graces which reflect honour upon God's name, you are continuing your praises in the best manner. Remember that with Christians to labour is to pray, and that there is much truth in the verse of Coleridge—

> " He prayeth best who loveth best."

To desire my fellow creatures' good and to seek after it, to desire God's glory, and so to live as to promote it, is the truest of devotion. The devotion of the cloisters is by no means equal to that of the man who is engaged in the battle of life ; the devotion of the nunnery and the monastery is at best the heroism of a soldier who shuns the battle; but the devotion of the man in business life, who turns all to the glory of God, is the courage of one who seeks the thickest of the fray, and there bears aloft the grand old standard of Jehovah-nissi. You need not be afraid that there is anything in any lawful calling that need make you desist from vital prayer; but, oh ! if your calling is such that you cannot pray in it, you had better leave it. If it be a sinful calling, an unholy calling, of course, you cannot present that to God, but any of the ordinary avocations of life are such that if you cannot sanctify them, it is a want of sanctity in yourself, and the fault lies with you. Men ought *always* to pray. It means that when they are using the lapstone, or the chisel, when the hands are on the plough handles, or on the spade, when they are measuring out the goods, when they are dealing in stocks, whatever they are doing, they are to turn all these things into a part of the sacred pursuit of God's glory. Their common garments are to be vestments, their meals are to be sacraments, their ordinary actions are to be sacrifices, and they themselves a royal priesthood, a peculiar people zealous for good works.

A third meaning which I think our Lord intended to convey to us was this: men ought always to pray, that is, *they should persevere in prayer.* This is probably his first meaning. When we ask God for a mercy once, we are not to consider that now we are not further to trouble him with it, but we are to come to him again and again. If we have asked of him seven times, we ought to continue until seventy times seven. In temporal mercies there may be a limit, and the Holy Ghost may bid us ask no more. Then must we say, the "Lord's will be done." If it be anything for our own personal advantage, we must let the Spirit of submission rule us, so that after having sought the Lord thrice, we shall be content with the promise, "My grace is sufficient for thee," and no longer ask that the thorn in the flesh should be removed. But in spiritual mercies, and especially in the united prayers of a church, there is no taking a denial. Here, if we would prevail, we must persist; we must continue incessantly and constantly, and know no pause to our prayer till we win the mercy to the fullest possible extent. "Men ought always to pray." Week by week, month by month, year by year; the conversion of that dear child is to be the father's main plea. The bringing in of that unconverted husband is to lie upon the wife's heart night and day till she gets it; she is not to take even ten or twenty years of unsuccessful prayer as a reason why she should cease; she is to set God no times nor seasons, but so long as there is life in her and life in the dear object of her solicitude, she is to continue still to plead with the mighty God of Jacob. The pastor is not to seek a blessing on his people occasionally, and then in receiving a measure of it to desist from further intercession, but he is to continue vehemently without pause, without restraining his energies, to cry aloud and spare not till the windows of heaven be opened and a blessing be given too large for him to house. But, brethren, how many times we ask of God, and have not because we do not wait long enough at the door! we knock a time or two at the gate of mercy, and as no friendly messenger opens the door, we go our ways. Too many prayers are like boys' runaway knocks, given, and then the giver is away before the door can be opened. O for grace to stand foot to foot with the angel of God, and never, never, never relax our hold ; feeling that the cause we plead is one in which we must be successful, for souls depend on it, the glory of God is connected with it, the state of our fellow men is in jeopardy. If we could have given up in prayer our own lives and the lives of those dearest to us, yet the souls of men we *cannot* give up, we must urge and plead again and again until we obtain the answer.

> " The humble suppliant cannot fail
>   To have his wants supplied,
> Since he for sinners intercedes
>   Who once for sinners died."

I cannot leave this part of the subject without observing that our Lord would have us learn that *men should be more frequent in prayer.* Not only should they always have the spirit of prayer, and make their whole lives a prayer, and persevere in any one object which is dear to their souls, but there should be a greater frequency of prayer amongst all the saints. I gather that from the parable, " lest by her continual coming she weary me." Prayerfulness will scarcely be kept up long unless you set apart times and seasons for prayer. There are no times laid down in Scripture except by the example of holy men, for the Lord trusts much to the love of his people and to the spontaneous motions of the inner life. He does not say, " Pray at seven o'clock in the morning every day," or " pray at night at eight, or nine, or ten, or eleven ;" but says, " Pray without ceasing." Yet every Christian will find it exceedingly useful to have his regular times for retirement, and I doubt whether any eminent piety can be maintained without these seasons being very carefully and scrupulously observed. We read in the old traditions of James the apostle, that he prayed so much that his knees grew hard through his long kneeling : and it is recorded by Fox, that Latimer, during the time of his imprisonment, was so much upon his knees that frequently the poor old man could not rise to his meals, and had to be lifted up by his servants. When he could no longer preach, and was immured within stone walls, his prayers went up to heaven for his country, and we in these times are receiving the blessing. Daniel prayed with his windows open daily and at regular intervals. " Seven times a day," saith one, " will I praise thee." David declared that at " Evening, and morning, and at noon," would he wait upon God. O that our intervals of prayer were not so distant one from the other ; would God that on the pilgrimage of life the wells at which we drink were more frequent. In this way should we continue in prayer.

Our Lord means, to sum up the whole, that *believers should exercise a universality of supplication*—we ought to pray at all times. There are no canonical hours in the Christian's day or week. We should pray from cockcrowing to midnight, at such times as the Spirit moveth us. We should pray in all estates, in our poverty and in our wealth, in our health and in our sickness, in the bright days of festival and in the dark nights of lamentation. We should pray at the birth and pray at the funeral, we should pray when our soul is glad within us by reason of abundant mercy, and we should pray when our soul draweth nigh unto the gates of death by reason of heaviness. We should pray in all transactions, whether secular or religious. Prayer should sanctify everything. The word of God and prayer should come in over and above the common things of daily life. Pray over a bargain, pray over going into the shop and coming out again. Remember in the days of Joshua how the Gibeonites deceived Israel because Israel enquired not of the Lord, and be not thou deceived by a specious temptation, as thou mayst well be if thou dost not daily come to the Lord, and say, "Guide me: make straight a plain path for my feet, and lead me in the way everlasting." Thou shalt never err by praying too much, thou shalt never make a mistake by asking God's guidance too often; but thou shalt find this to be the gracious illumination of thine eyes, if in the turning of the road where two paths meet which seem to be equally right, thou shalt stay a moment and cry unto God, "Guide me, O thou great Jehovah." "Men ought always to pray." I have enlarged upon it from this pulpit, go you and expound it in your daily lives.

II. In enforcing this precept, our Lord gives us a parable in which there are TWO ACTORS, the characteristics of the two actors being such as to add strength to his precept.

In the first verse of the parable there is *a judge*. Now, herein is the great advantage to us in prayer. Brethren, if this poor woman prevailed with a judge whose office is stern, unbending, untender, how much more ought you and I to be instant in prayer and hopeful of success when we have to supplicate a Father! Far other is a father than a judge. The judge must necessarily be impartial, stern, but the father is necessarily partial to his child, compassionate and tender to his own offspring. Doth she prevail over a judge; and shall not we prevail with our Father who is in heaven? And doth she continue in her desperate need to weary him until she wins what she desires; and shall not we continue in the agony of our desires until we get from our heavenly Father whatsoever his word hath promised?

In addition to being a judge, he was *devoid of all good character*. In both branches he failed. He "feared not God." Conscience was seared in him, he had no thoughts of the great judgment-seat before which judges must appear. Though possibly he had taken an oath before God to judge impartially, yet he forgot his oath, and trod justice under his foot. "Neither did he regard man." The approbation of his fellow creatures, which is very often a power, even with naturally bad men, either to restrain them from overt evil, or else to constrain them to righteousness, this principle had no effect upon him. Now, if the widow prevailed over such a wretch as this, if the iron of her importunity broke the iron and steel of this man's obduracy, how much more may we expect to be successful with him who is righteous, and just, and good, the Friend of the needy, the Father of the fatherless, and the Avenger of all such as are oppressed! O let the character of God as it rises before you in all its majesty of truthfulness and faithfulness, blended with lovingkindness, and tenderness, and mercy, excite in you an indefatigable ardour of supplication, making you resolve with this poor woman that you will never cease to supplicate until you win your suit.

The judge was a man so unutterably bad, that he *even confessed his badness to himself*, with great contentment too. Without the slightest tinge of remorse, he said within himself, " Though I fear not God, neither regard man." There are few sinners who will go this length. They may neither fear God nor regard men, yet still they will indulge in their minds some semblance of that which is virtuous, and cheat themselves into the belief that at least they are not worse than others. But with this man there was no self-deception. He was as cool about this avowal as the Pharisee was concerning the opposite, " God, I thank thee that I am not as other men are." To what a brazen impertinence must this man have come, to what an extent must he have hardened his mind, that knowing himself to be such, he yet climbed the judgment-seat, and sat there to judge his fellow men! Yet the woman prevailed with this monster in human form, who had come to take pleasure in his own wickedness, and gloated in the badness of his own heart. Over this man importunity prevailed—how much more over him who spared not his own Son, but freely delivered him up for us all; how much more over him whose name is love, whose nature is everything that is attractive and encouraging to such as seek his face! The worse this judge appears, and he could scarcely have been painted in blacker colours, the more does the voice of the Saviour seem to say to us, " Men ought always to pray, and not to faint."

Note with regard to the character of this judge, that he was one who *consciously cared for nothing but his own ease.* When at last he consented to do justice, the only motive which moved him, was, " lest by her continual coming she weary me. " She *stun* me," might be the Greek word—a kind of slang, I suppose, of that period, meaning lest "she batter me," "she bruise me," and as some translate it, "black my face with her incessant constant batterings." That was the kind of language he used; a short quick sentence of indignation at being bothered, as we should say, by such a case as this. The only thing that moved him was a desire to be at ease, and to take things comfortably. O brethren, if she could prevail over such a one, how much more shall we speed with God whose delight it is to take care of his children, who loves them even as the apple of his eye!

This judge was *practically unkind and cruel* to her; yet the widow continued. For awhile he would not listen to her, though her household, her life, her children's comfort, were all hanging upon his will; he left her by a passive injustice to suffer still. But our God has been practically kind and gracious to us, up to this moment he has heard us and granted our requests. Set this against the character of the judge, and surely every loving heart that knows the power of prayer will be moved to incessant importunity.

We must, however, pass on now to notice the other actor in the scene — *the widow;* and here everything tells again the same way, to induce the church of God to be importunate. She was apparently *a perfect stranger to the judge.* She appeared before him as an individual in whom he took no interest. He had possibly never seen her before; who she was and what she wanted was no concern to him. But when the church appears before God she comes as Christ's own bride, she appears before the Father as one whom he has loved with an everlasting love. And shall he not avenge his own elect, his own chosen, his own people? Shall not their prayers prevail with him, when a stranger's importunity won a suit of an unwilling judge?

The widow appeared at the judgment-seat *without a friend.* According to the parable, she had no advocate, no powerful pleader to stand up in the court and say, "I am the patron of this humble woman." If she prevailed, she must prevail by her own ardour and her own intensity of purpose. But when you and I come before our Father, we come not alone, for—

"He is at the Father's side,
The Man of love, the Crucified."

We have a Friend who ever liveth to make intercession for us. O Christian, urge thy suit with holy boldness, press thy case, for the blood of Jesus speaks with a voice that must be heard. Be not thou therefore faint in thy spirit, but continue instant in thy supplication.

This poor woman came *without a promise to encourage her,* nay, with the reverse, with much to discourage; but when you and I come before God, we are commanded to pray by God himself, and we are promised that if we ask it shall be given us, if we seek we shall find. Does she win without the sacred weapon of the promise, and shall not we win who can set the battering-rams of God's own word against the gates of heaven, a battering-ram that shall make every timber in those gates to quiver? O brethren, we must not pause nor cease a moment while we have God's promise to back our plea.

The widow, in addition to having no promise whatever, was even *without the right of constant access.* She had, I suppose, a right to clamour to be heard at ordinary times when judgment was administered, but what right had she to dog the judge's footsteps, to waylay him in the streets, to hammer at his private door, to be heard calling at nightfall, so that he, sleeping at the top of his house, was awakened by her cries? She had no permission so to importune, but we may come to God at all times and all seasons. We may cry day and night unto him, for he has bidden us pray without ceasing. What, without a permit is this woman so incessant! and with the sacred permissions which God has given us, and the encouragement of abounding lovingkindness, shall we cease to plead?

She, poor soul, every time she prayed, *provoked the judge;* lines of anger were on his face. I doubt not he foamed at the mouth to think he should be wearied by a person so insignificant; but with Jesus, every time we plead we please him rather than provoke him. The prayers of the saints are the music of God's ears.

> " To him there's music in a groan,
> And beauty in a tear."

We, speaking after the manner of men, bring a gratification to God when we intercede with him. He is vexed with us if we restrain our supplications; he is pleased with us when we draw near constantly. Oh, then, as you see the smile upon the Father's face, children of his love, I beseech you faint not, but continue still without ceasing to entreat the blessing.

Once more, this woman had a suit in which *the judge could not be himself personally interested;* but ours is a case in which the God we plead with is more interested than we are; for when a church asks for the conversion of souls, she may justly say, " Arise, O God, plead thine own cause." It is for the honour of Christ that souls should be converted; it brings glory to the mercy and power of God when great sinners are turned from the error of their ways; consequently we are pleading for the Judge with the Judge, for God we are pleading with God. Our prayer is virtually *for* Christ as *through* Christ, that his kingdom may come, and his will may be done.

I must not forget to mention that in this woman's case *she was only one.* She prevailed though she was only one, but shall not God avenge his own elect, who are not *one,* but tens of thousands? If there be a promise that if two or three are agreed it shall be done, how much more if in any church hundreds meet together with unanimous souls anxiously desiring that God would fulfil his promise? These pleas cast chains around the throne of God! How do they, as it were, hem in omnipotence! How they constrain the Almighty to arise out of his place and come in answer to his people, and do the great deed which shall bless his church and glorify himself.

You see, then, whether we consider the judge, or consider the widow, each character has points about it which tend to make us see our duty and our privilege to pray without ceasing.

III. The third and last point: THE POWER WHICH, ACCORDING TO THIS PARABLE, TRIUMPHED.

This power was not the woman's eloquence, "I pray thee avenge me of mine adversary." These words are. very few. They have the merit of being very expressive, but he that would study oratory will not gather many lessons from them. "I pray thee avenge me of mine adversary." Just eight words. You observe there is no plea, there is nothing about her widowhood, nothing urged about her children, nothing said about the wickedness of her adversary, nothing concerning the judgment of God upon unjust judges, nor about the wrath of God upon unjust men, who devour widows' houses—nothing of the kind. "I pray thee avenge me of mine adversary." Her success, therefore, did not depend upon her power in rhetoric, and we learn from this that the prevalence of a soul or of a church with God does not rest upon the elocution of its words, or upon the eloquence of its language. The prayer which mounts to heaven may have but very few of the tail feathers of adornment about it, but it must have the strong wing feathers of intense desire; it must not be as the peacock, gorgeous for beauty, but it must be as the eagle, for soaring aloft, if it would ascend up to the seventh heavens. When you pray in public, as a rule the shorter the better. Words are cumbersome to prayer. It often happens that an abundance of words reveals a scarcity of desires. Verbiage is generally nothing better in prayer than a miserable fig leaf with which to cover the nakedness of an unawakened soul.

Another thing is quite certain, namely, that the woman *did not prevail through the merits of her case.* It may have been a very good case, there is nothing said about that. I do not doubt the right-ness of it; but still, the judge did not know nor care whether it was right or wrong; all he cared about was, this woman troubled him. He does not say, "She has a good case, and I ought to listen to it." No, he was too bad a man to be moved by such a motive—but "she worries me," that is all, "I will attend to it." So in our suit—in the suit of a sinner with God, it is not the merit of his case that can ever prevail with God. Thou hast no merit. If thou art to win, another's merit must stand instead of thine, and on thy part it must not be merit but misery; it must not be thy righteousness but thy importunity that is to prevail with God. How this ought to encourage those of you who are labouring under a sense of unworthiness! However unworthy you may be, continue in prayer. Black may be the hand, but if it can but lift the knocker, the gate will open. Ay, though thou have a palsy in that hand; though, in addition to that palsy, thou be leprous, and the white leprosy be on thy forehead, yet if thou canst but tremblingly lift up that knocker and let it fall by its own weight upon that sacred promise, thou shalt surely get an audience with the King of kings. It is not eloquence, it is not merit, that wins with God, it is nothing but importunity.

Note with regard to this woman, that the judge said first, she troubled him, next he said, she came continually, and then he added his fear lest "she weary me." I think the case was somewhat after this fashion. The judge was sitting one morning on his bench, and many were the persons coming before him asking justice, which he was dealing out with the impartiality of a villain, giving always his best word to him who brought the heaviest bribes; when presently a poor woman uttered her plaint. She had tried to be heard several times, but her voice had been drowned by others, but this time it was more shrill and sharp, and she caught the judge's eye. "My lord, avenge me of mine adversary." He no sooner sees from her poverty-stricken dress that there are no bribes to be had, than he replies, "Hold your tongue! I have other business to attend to." He goes on with another suit in which the fees were more attractive. Still he hears the cry again, "My lord, I am a widow, avenge me of mine adversary." Vexed with the renewed disturbance, he bade the usher put her out, because she interrupted the silence of the court and stopped the public business. "Take care she does not get in again to-morrow," said he, "she is a troublesome woman." Long ere the morrow had come, he found out the truth of his opinion. She waited till he left the court, dogged his footsteps, and followed him through the streets, until he was glad to get through his door, and bade the servants fasten it lest that noisy widow should come in, for she had constantly assailed him with the cry, "Avenge me of mine adversary." He is now safely within doors, and bids the servants bring in his meal. They are pouring water on his hands and feet, his lordship is about to enjoy his repast, when a heavy knock is heard at the door, followed by a clamour, pushing, and a scuffle. "What is it?" saith he. "It is a woman outside, a widow woman, who wants your lordship to see justice done her." "Tell her I cannot attend to her, she must be gone." He seeks his rest at nightfall on the housetop, when he hears a heavy knock at the door, and a voice comes up from the street beneath his residence, "My lord, avenge me of mine adversary." The next morning his court is open, and, though she is forbidden to enter, like a dog that will enter some-how, she finds her way in, and she interrupts the court continually with her plea, "My lord, avenge me of mine adversary." Ask her why she is thus importunate, and she will tell you her husband is dead, and he left a little plot of land—it was all they had, and a cruel neighbour who looked with greedy eyes upon that little plot, has taken it as Ahab took Naboth's vineyard, and now she is without any meal or any oil for the little ones, and they are crying for food. Oh, if their father had been alive, how he would have guarded their interests! but she has no helper, and the case is a glaring one; and what is a judge for if he is not to protect the injured? She has no other chance, for the creditor is about to take away her children to sell them into bondage. She cannot bear that. "No," she says, "I have but one chance; it is that this man should speak up for me and do me justice, and I have made up my mind he shall never rest till he does so. I am resolved that if I perish, the last words on my lips shall be, 'Avenge me of mine adversary.'" So the court is continually interrupted. Again the judge shouts, "Put her out; put her out! I cannot conduct the business at all with this crazy woman here continually dinning in my ears a shriek of 'Avenge me of mine adversary.'" But it is sooner said than done. She lays hold of the pillars of the court so as not to be dragged out, and when at last they get her in the street, she does but wait her chance to enter again, she pursues the judge along the highways, she never lets him have a minute's peace. "Well," says the judge, "I am worried out of my very life. I care not for the widow, nor her property, nor her children; let them starve, what are they to me? but I cannot stand this, it will weary me beyond measure. I will see to it." It is done, and she goes her way. Nothing but her importunity prevails.

Now, brethren, you have many other weapons to use with God in prayer, but our Saviour bids you not neglect this master, all-conquering, instrument of importunity. God will be more easily moved than this unjust judge, only be you as importunate as this widow was. If you are sure it is a right thing for which you are asking, plead now, plead at noon, plead at night, plead on; with cries and tears spread out your case, order your arguments, back up your pleas with reasons, urge the precious blood of Jesus, set the wounds of Christ before the Father's eyes, bring out the atoning sacrifice, point to Calvary, enlist the crowned Prince, the Priest who stands at the right hand of God; and resolve in your very soul that if Zion do not flourish, if souls be not saved, if your family be not blessed, if your own zeal be not revived, yet you will die with the plea upon your lips, and with the importunate wish upon your spirits. Let me tell you that if any of you should die with your prayers unanswered, you need not conclude that God has disappointed you. With one story I will finish. I have heard that a certain godly father had the unhappiness to be the parent of some five or six most graceless sons. All of them as they grew up imbibed infidel sentiments, and led a libidinous life. The father who had been constantly praying for them, and was a pattern of every virtue, hoped at least that in his death he might be able to say a word that should move their hearts. He gathered them to his bedside, but his unhappiness in dying was extreme, for he lost the light of God's countenance, and was beset with doubts and fears, and the last black thought that haunted him was, "Instead of my death being a testimony for God, which will win my dear sons, I die in such darkness and gloom that I fear I shall confirm them in their infidelity, and lead them to think that there is nothing in Christianity at all." The effect was the reverse. The sons came round the grave at the funeral, and when they returned to the house, the eldest son thus addressed his brothers :—"My brothers, throughout his lifetime, our father often spoke to us about religion, and we have always despised it, but what a sermon his deathbed has been to us! for if he who served God so well and lived so near to God found it so hard a thing to die, what kind of death may we expect ours to be who have lived without God and without hope?" The same feeling possessed them all, and thus the father's death had strangely answered the prayers of his life through the grace of God. You cannot tell but what, when you are in glory, you should look down from the windows of heaven and receive a double heaven in beholding your dear sons and daughters converted by the words you left behind. I do not say this to make you cease pleading for their immediate conversion, but to encourage you. Never give up prayer, never be tempted to cease from it. So long as there is breath in your body, and breath in their bodies, continue still to pray, for I tell you that he will avenge you speedily though he bear long with you. God bless these words for Jesus' sake. Amen.

Timely Reflections

"Now is our salvation nearer than when we believed."—Romans xiii. 11.

But what "salvation" is this? The question is important because we very commonly speak of "salvation" as that state of grace into which every one that believes in Jesus is introduced when he passes from death unto life, being delivered from the power of darkness, and translated into the kingdom of God's dear Son. This sweet assurance we celebrate in our hymns of praise—

> "The moment a sinner believes,
> And trusts in his crucified God;
> His pardon at once he receives,
> Redemption in full through his blood."

Salvation, so far as the forgiveness of sin, the imputation of righteousness, and the eternal safety of the soul are concerned, is given to us the moment that we are brought to trust in Jesus. But the term "salvation" here, and in some other parts of Scripture, signifies that complete deliverance from sin, that glorious perfection, which will not be attained by us until the day of the appearing of our Lord and Saviour Jesus Christ. Salvation here signifies entire deliverance from indwelling sin, perfect sanctification; and, as I take it, includes the resurrection of the body and the glorification of body and soul with Christ Jesus in the world to come. Salvation here means what many think it always implies, namely, eternal glory. At this hour our perfect salvation is nearer than when we believed.

Observe the date from which the apostle begins to reckon. He does not say our salvation is nearer than when we were christened; that is a ceremony of which the apostle never dreamt, a tradition and invention of men which had never crossed his mind. He does not say your salvation is nearer than when you were confirmed; that also was a thing quite unknown to him. He does not reckon even from our baptism; as if he were to say, now is your salvation nearer than when you put on Christ openly in baptism. But he strikes at the vital point; he specifies the true indication of spiritual life, namely, "believe." What could ever come of all that is before believing? It is all death; it is not worth reckoning. No matter how studied the ceremony, how garnished with profession, up to the moment a man believes, he has no spiritual life, he comes not into the happiness of the living, neither has the apostle aught to say to him, except that he is dead in trespasses and sins. The moment of faith is the moment from which he dates his spiritual career. It is when we look to Jesus hanging upon the cross, our substitute, that life comes to us. As we look we live, we look and are forgiven, we look and are saved; and from that time forward with our faces Zionward we start upon the celestial pilgrimage towards that glorious city which hath foundations, whose builder and maker is God.

Thus it was, then, that the apostle measured from one fixed point to another fixed point. If you have two shifting points you cannot say, now are you nearer this or that. If the time of our believing was not a fixed and definite moment, but a thing which may be put here or there, we could not reckon from that; and if the time of our emancipation from this body and our complete salvation were unsettled, precarious, a point that moves, a sort of planetary star, we could not say we are getting any nearer to it. But the apostle takes a fixed point. There is a man saved; he has believed in Christ. That day he believed in Christ, ay, that very minute, he may not know what minute, but God knows, that very second, at that tick of the clock in which he trusted in Christ, he became a new man, old things were passed away, and all things became new. Henceforth that is a fixed and definite point in that man's history from which to date. And there is another point, settled by God in the divine decree, never to be removed, neither to be ante-dated nor post-dated, a moment when those that believe shall be with Christ where he is, and shall be like him, and shall behold his glory for ever.

Now, between these two points you and I, if we have believed, are sailing; and this evening at the close of the year it seemed meet for me to haul up the log, and just to note where we are on the sea that rolls between these two blessed points, and to congratulate my fellow believers, that now to-night we are nearer the eternal port by the space of many years than when we first slipped our cable, hauled up the anchor, and began to sail towards the haven of everlasting rest. "Now is our salvation nearer than when we believed."

I have been told—I have not been the voyage—but I have been told that in going to Australia it has frequently been the custom to toast "Friends behind," till they get half way; and then it changes, "Friends ahead." "Here's to the helm, friends behind," and then anon to the port, "Friends ahead." Well, I am going to say something to-night about *things behind,* and then we shall congratulate you as we talk of *things ahead.* " Now is our salvation nearer than when we believed."

I. THE THINGS THAT ARE BEHIND. I want you to look back a little, all of you who have started from the point of believing.

Recollect—and it will do you good to recollect it—when you did believe. Oh, that blessed day! Of all the days we have ever seen, that was, in some respects, the brightest of all. Not to be compared with the day of our natural birth, for that was a day of our first weeping, but in the day of our new birth, we wept tears of sacred joy; we were thrust from death into life, from condemnation to acceptance, from everlasting peril into eternal safety.

> " Happy day, happy day !
> When Jesus wash'd my sins away !"

That was the day, we may say, when we left the first shore; and you know all those who are going round the world to the other side to dwell, always look back with great satisfaction at the day when they left. When the vessel was first tugged out of dock and safely towed down to the Nore, and began to try the deep sea wave, what congratulations there were of friends—and many tears, no doubt, and waving of handkerchiefs, and hurrahing, as the vessel left the port. Well, now, in our case we remember how our friends and kinsfolk in Christ rejoiced over us ; how glad they were to hear us tell the tale of saving grace ! They prized us as a new-born child is prized in the household. Nay, not only friends below, but the angels looking down from heaven rejoiced over us as repenting sinners. And surely if it were worth their while to rejoice when we believed, we need not blush to go back to that period. It is not very long with some of you—well, be grateful. It is a long time with some of you. Some of us can, no doubt, count twenty years since first we knew the Lord ! Happy years they have been, too ! And happy was that day when we became first enlisted in his service; when we first left the shores of earth to try and find the new country, the better land Yes, " when we believed ; " we will dwell upon that time, and let our souls ring the sweet silver bells of gratitude as we bless the Lord that we were not left to perish in our natural unbelief, but that we have believed in Christ Jesus.

Since then—now turn to your logs—since then we have had a good number of storms. I remember that first storm we had in that Bay of Biscay—for there is generally such a bay as that soon after the mariner gets off from shore. What a tempest it was ! We had not long rejoiced before all our rejoicing was gone. We had not long found Christ before we thought that Satan himself had found us. We fancied it was all a delusion ; we were ready to give up our confidence. We had thought at first that the moment we believed there would be an end of conflict ; but we discovered that it was then the conflict began; and perhaps one of the severest storms our vessel has ever had was just at the first. You remember it. And we have had many since then, when the waves of unbelief have made us stand and tremble. You have seen one washed overboard that you thought very dear. You have yourselves suffered loss, and endured great peril. You were glad to get some of your treasures; "But there," said you, "let the ingots go." Now the ship rights! Happy were you if you might, by losing earthly substances and carnal joys, find peace and safety in Christ. You remember, too, when you had to sail very slowly in the thick fog, and keep the whistle always sounding. And see the look-out you had to keep at the bows, for fear you should run into something and come to mischief. And you remember when you had almost gone, and you just caught sight of the red lights, for if you had but gone a little further your soul would have been wrecked, cast away for ever. But mercy interposed at the precise moment, when there was time yet to tack about and save the vessel, and rescued us in the hour of temptation, saved us as by fire.

Well, now, why do I call these things to your remembrance, but to make you bless the name of your God. You have been nearly ship-wrecked, but you are not wrecked. The storm has been very furious, but above all the billows Jehovah's power has kept and preserved you. Your feet had almost gone, your steps had well nigh slipped, but the divine power interposed in everlasting grace, and to this day—a wonder unto many, but especially a wonder to yourself—you are still on the road towards the celestial city, and you are nearer to it than when you first believed.

But I would not have your recollection of what is behind be altogether saddened. Remember, beloved, you have had a great deal of fair weather, too, since you left the port of believing. Oh, there have been happy days with us! Blessed days, as the days of heaven upon earth. We have sailed along with a favouring breeze; all has been happy within our spirits; and peace, like a river, has abounded in our souls. Let us praise the name of God for this. Life is not the dreary thing that some men say it is. It hath its sorrows, for what rose hath not its thorns? Thistles spring up in it, but withal, who would not expect the thistles to grow here and there in the midst of a harvest field? But we bear our testimony that we have not had such a bad time of it after all;

> "The men of grace have found
> Glory begun below,
> Celestial fruit on earthly ground,
> From faith and hope may grow."

So that behind us, since the hour we first believed, there are the storms from which we have escaped, but there are also the mercies, the lovingkindnesses which we dare not and will not forget.

Behind us, too, dear brethren—and this will be a mingled thought—

behind us, how many opportunities of service have we left? When we sailed ourselves, there were with us many other little ships, and some of these—ah! some of these, have been cast away and shipwrecked before our eyes. In that night of storm, when we ourselves were hard beset, a companion vessel, that bade fair to make as good a voyage as our own, went to pieces and was never heard of more; a great professor foundered, his hypocrisy was discovered, and his profession ruined for ever. Another, who seemed to be as ardent for the cause of Christ as we, passed away, stranded on simple pleasures, broken to pieces on the rocks of worldliness and lost—and we preserved! Blessed be God, we are preserved! But we have had many opportunities of seeking out the distressed, of bringing some of the shipwrecked ones to safety. Did we always do it? Well, I hope there are many of you who, during past years, have been the means of bringing some to Christ. I know many of you have, but I fear some of you have not. Just before this sermon commenced I saw one who wished to make a profession of her faith in Christ, and she traced her conversion, she said, to the prayers of one of our members. I dare say you would know him if I were to mention his name—a humble brother; and I was so thankful to think that God should bless his prayer in the family to the conversion of one who had listened to him. May all of us be looking out for others, and endeavouring to bring them to Christ. But what a sad thing it is if we have to recollect that in our sailing that night we rescued none from the storm: if we are compelled to say, " I saw the signals go up, I know they were firing minute-guns of distress, but I passed them by, I never sent aid there; and whether they were saved or lost I do not know. I had enough to do to look to myself; I never looked to them." During this year hundreds have gone to their graves; some of your own children perhaps, or neighbours; are you clear of their blood? Are you clear of their blood? It would be an awful piece of brutality if a boat full of poor shipwrecked mariners, far out at sea, saw a vessel in the offing, and yet that vessel would not turn aside to help them. But that is the conduct of many professors of Christ; they see others perishing, but they will not tell them the way of salvation; they neither pray for them, nor labour for them; but they let them go down to hell unwept, unpitied, and uncared for. Where are your bowels of compassion, professor, that you have done this? Perhaps you have done it; if so, do not merely regret, but earnestly amend.

We ought to recollect again, that since we left the fixed point of believing, and began to voyage onward towards the point of glory, we have had many opportunities of serving the Lord Jesus, and, I may ask, have we always availed ourselves of them? I wish we had sung as many hymns for Christ as he deserved. O that I could have put upon his head the crown which he deserves to have of his poor servant, whom he has delivered out of bondage and made to rejoice in liberty! O that I had always spoken up for his name; that I had poured a broadside into his enemies whenever I had an opportunity. We can sometimes sing—

> " Is there a lamb amongst the flock,
>   I would disdain to feed;
>   Is there a foe before whose face,
>   I fear thy cause to plead?"

And though we sing it, and mean it, yet I fear many of the lambs are not fed, and before many a foe we do not plead the cause of Christ. Golden opportunities of bringing glory to Christ are suffered to go by. Alas! for this. If we could weep in heaven we might weep the loss of such opportunities; but instead of weeping, let us earnestly pray that for the future we may serve the Master with heart, and soul, and strength, so long as we have any being.

II. Thus much about things behind; and now, very briefly indeed, ANTICIPATION OF THOSE WHO ARE AHEAD, AND OF THE THINGS THAT ARE AHEAD.

Keeping our look out, expecting to see other storms, and soon to reach a fairer clime, what is there which we are expecting?

I cannot fail to expect more storms between this and the fair haven. There shall be more blustering winds and tossing billows. It is not over yet. It was not all smooth behind; it cannot be all smooth before. But there is this to be said—though there may be many more storms, they must be fewer in number than they were. There cannot be so many, for so many have already gone. As we are nearer home, therefore so many the fewer trials have we to bear. You are getting through them, Christian. Every one, as you pass it, leaves one the less. Be comforted, then, be comforted. And how few storms must remain for some of you? "I am on the better side of seventy," said one. "Why," said another, "I thought you were seventy-seven." "So I am," said he, " and that is the right side of seventy; it is the nearest side home." Can you not trust God for the next half-dozen years? You will not have more than that perhaps. You cannot expect to have twenty. He has helped you for seventy—will he not help you for another ten? Will he change at the last? Has he hitherto taught you to trust in his name, and brought you so far to put you to shame? Has he finished the house all but the last course of bricks, and will he not complete it in due course? Surely he will. Be of good courage. There are few storms, after all, that are ahead, to those that have passed through many already. The further we are on the road, the less there is of it to bear.

Beloved, there will be fairer winds yet, thank God. We cannot suspect it will be all storms. It would be folly to suppose there would be none; it would be greater folly still to suppose it would be all boisterous weather. Before we reach the heavenly plains, or walk the golden streets, there is a land called Beulah, which John Bunyan pictures in his " Pilgrim's Progress," and surely it is no realm of fancy. In old age God's people are often brought into a peaceable frame of mind, where their confidences are always bright, their enjoyment of Christ always great ; where they have not those molestations which afflicted them when they were young; they have come to perfect peace and rest. We can expect this, and we will steer on towards it. There are calm days ahead. Christ will be with us ; our communion with him shall be sweet. Do you know, I look forward in days to come to the oft-recurring refreshment of our Sabbaths. If we are to be spared there will always be these oases in the desert. Though we have some of us our hardest day's work, and often wish we could sit in a pew and hear somebody else, yet there is no day like the Sabbath after all. Oh, what a blessed help it is to heaven ! If we had not those windows, the earth would be a blank indeed. But with these sacred windows, that which would otherwise be a hard black wall, shutting out all light, becomes a very palace, and we look through these windows up to the better palace, where the eternal Sabbath shall be our portion. Well, there are these Sabbaths ahead, there is the outpouring of the Spirit ; there are covenant blessings to be participated, and there is the safety which providential grace can bring, all lying ahead of us. Let us, then, be comforted, and pass on.

And there will be more opportunities ahead. Now, you young people especially should be looking out. I spoke of occasions of serving God which we had wasted. Do not let us waste any more, but gird up the loins of our lives. Let this be our prayer, that we may snatch every opportunity by the wing—take time by the forelock; and, in the service of God, contend with might and main for the truth. The wheels of eternity are sounding behind us ; life must be short. To those to whom it is longest it is but brief. Work on, worker ! You have scarce time to finish your day's work. Waste not a second. Throw not away these priceless hours. Speed ! speed ! speed ! as with sevenfold wing it glides forward—swifter than the thunderbolt. Oh, pause not ! trifle not. O Christian, if thou wouldst take thy crowns up to thy Lord, and great sheaves from the harvest, " work while it is called to-day, for the night cometh wherein no man can work." "It is high time," says our apostle, " to awake out of sleep." Would that you would consider it. Be not as those who open their eyes in the morning only to close them again, like the sluggard with the reflection, " I need not bestir myself just yet." But start, man, from thy slumbers as one who feels that he has slept too long, and must now briskly cast off dull sloth, bestirring himself with eager haste to do his appointed task, to redeem the time, to reclaim the golden hours. For, consider this, thy calling is of God, and the King's business requireth haste.

But looking still further ahead, let us to-night, when we remember we are nearer our salvation than when we believed, begin to think of what that salvation will be. How near it may be to some of us it were not possible for us to tell. But twenty-four hours may take some of us there—ay, less time than that. What is the distance between earth and heaven? It only takes a second of time.

> "One gentle sigh, the fetter breaks—
> We scarce can say 'They're gone!'
> Before the willing spirit takes
> Her mansion near the throne."

Now, what shall we see when we get there? Well, first we shall see Jesus. And the sight of him, oh! say no more—think of it. The vision of the Man of Sorrows; our Beloved, who gave himself for us—once to see him, once to fall at his feet, and speechless there to lie—bursting with gratitude, which even there shall be inexpressible. Oh, what a heaven to be with him! Then, next to Jesus, we shall be with all the bright spirits that have gone before us. Those that go to Australia begin forgetting father and mother that they left behind, because they are thinking of the brother and sister that went before. They will be at the landing-place to meet them. Some of you have dear children that went home in infancy; some of you have a dear wife or a husband, and they have been looking for you. I do not doubt they will know you. It will be one of the joys of heaven to reunite these broken ties. I do not think Rowland Hill was at all foolish when he rode over from Cambridge, a distance of thirteen miles, to see an old woman who was upon her dying bed. He said, "You are older than I am, but I am getting older, and, even now, I sometimes think they have forgotten me; but in the meantime, as you are going first, take my love to the four great Johns—John who leaned on Jesus' bosom, and John Bunyan, and John Calvin, and John Knox; take my love to them, and tell them poor old Rowly will be coming by-and-by." I cannot doubt but that the message would have been delivered. I think there is such a connection between earth and heaven that we shall see those who have gone before. How comfortable it must be to some aged ones, when they think that though they be taken from that part of the family which remains on earth, they have a larger family circle probably in heaven than here! It was so with a poor old man who accosted me the other day in a country lane, and asked me for something. As I gave to him I said, "How is it you are so poor?" "Ah!" he said, "everybody is dead that ever cared for me." "But," I said, "surely there is somebody left?" "No, sir," he said, "there is nobody; I buried my poor old wife last year; we had two or three children, and they all died; my brother had five or six, and they died years ago. The people that were young in my time, they are all gone; I do not know anybody now, nobody cares for me." So too wrote one, who, if I mistake not, had been a votary of fashion in her gay circles:

> " The friends of youth, manhood, and age,
>   At length are all laid in the ground;
> An unit I stand on life's stage,
>   With nothing but vanity round.
>
> I wander bewildered and lost,
>   Without impulse or interest view;
> And all hope of my heart is at most—
>   To soon bid the desert adieu.
>
> But this derelict state of man's lot,
>   That fate to the aged ordains,
> Bids the heart turn the thoughts where it ought,
>   Nor seek worldly cure for its pains.
>
> Thus I turn from the past and the lost,
>   Close the view my life's picture supplies ;
> And while penitent tears pay the cost,
>   Blot the follies of mirth from my eyes."

Well, but what a comfort to such a one if he could but feel that though there is nobody here, yet there are plenty there among those that are gone before to greet and love him ! So, let us salute those that are ahead. We cannot yet see the bright light at the harbour's mouth, but we know we are on the right tack, and that God's eternal spirit is driving us on towards the harbour. O let us still think of them, and sing as Wesley did—

> " E'en now by faith we join our hands
>   With those that went before ;
> And greet the blood-besprinkled bands
>   On the eternal shore."

I shall not delay you, however, with these anticipations. There are some mournful reflections with which I will close. The Lord Jesus, whose eyes of fire can read all hearts, knoweth this night that there are some of you who are not nearer your salvation than when you believed; because, first, you never did believe; and, secondly, that which you are nearer to is not salvation. Alas! alas! alas! is it true that you have not believed ? What does that mean? It means, with some of you that you have violated conscience. From your youth up you knew the beauties of godliness, and the brightness of a holy life; but you have chosen evil in defiance of the inward monitor. You have elected to be an enemy of God; you have not believed, and so have been a traitor to your own conscience. Despite that, you have done it in the face of a hundred warnings—hundreds, did I say! yea, hundreds of thousands of invitations. Are there not some of you who seem resolved to go to hell over a mother's tears and prayers? You are pressing forward in the wrong way, in defiance of the admonitions of a father who is now in heaven. A godly education trained you for the sky, but your own choice hath doomed you to another fate. Alas! there are many in this congregation who have done violence to the Holy Ghost also; who have been accused, convinced, startled, made to pray; and yet tears have been brushed away—they have plunged into gaiety; they have returned to thoughtlessness; and so the hour of grace, and the opportunity of mercy, they have flung to the winds. If I knew the private history of a good many who have seats in this tabernacle, it would be a dreadful story of striving against every good principle, not for their own good, but for their own evil. You have fought not with devils, but with angels. You have fought with angels, that you might be permitted to damn your own souls. You have contended with eternal mercy, and what for the crown of your victory, but that you might ruin yourselves for ever! If men were half as earnest to be saved, as many seem to be to be lost, it were a blessed change. But, oh! the strugglings of conscience, the murdering of godly thoughts, the putting of the bowstring about the neck of solemn conviction, which have been committed by some who are here! You have not believed—not believed! and here on this last Sunday night of 1868! Though three, four, five, six, or ten years ago you were promising to mend and look hopeful, here you are just the same, with this liable to be put upon you—*not believed, confirmed unbelievers, enemies to God.*

Well now, here comes this horrible thought across my mind, and I wish I did not feel compelled to utter it, but I must. Then, since you are not believing, your eternal destruction is nearer than ever it was. It must be so. Look at the vessel. The bows were in that direction; she is sailing that way. Cannot you see the trail she has left in the ocean? Do you not see everything indicates she is fast set towards that dreadful rock that shall grind her to pieces? It is not merely that the helm seems thus turned, but there is a current underneath the vessel which seems to be bearing it along swiftly. Apparently, the life of some of you is towards evil and towards hell. Your whole tenour of life seems to bear you that way; your inclinations, your companions, your very business, seem to have acted like a gulf stream to bear you on towards ruin. Besides that, the wind is blowing that way—that wind that blew you into the theatre last night, that blows you into carnal company, into the house of vice, that is drawing you fast, I say, into fierce temptations, while you grow more and more reckless of the consequences. What with the helm set and perpetually nailed fast, so that it should not be moved, a current under the vessel, and the wind filling her sails—great God, how is she speeding on towards her eternal fate! But, worst of all, there is the engine within throbbing, palpitating, helping the ship towards her ruin. Every thought, every desire you have, seems to be leading you away from Christ, and onward towards mischief. See there are others that have gone down during the past year; others have been wrecked—wrecked on those rocks to which you are determinedly steering your soul. The wind is getting up, the tempest is howling fiercer than ever! With some of you the sins you did not dare to do once have become common, and the things that made you shudder and your blood run cold, and you said, "Is thy servant a dog that he should do this thing?" you do them now. But the wind is still getting up, howling and blowing strong upon you, and driving you onward in that evil course which must end in your eternal destruction. The wind is getting up! If you look ahead you see the iron-bound coast before you. Iron-bound, I say, not a harbour or a creek—nothing to run to—not a crack or a crevice up which a man might climb; and you have no life-boat along that coast to rescue you, and no boats in your vessel that would prove seaworthy when the vessel strikes. O that God might preserve you from ever striking upon the rocks of destruction! Some of you are steering ahead fast for them. Hard aport! Turn the vessel round, for there is yet a chance! Stop her! Now she is right in the wind's teeth. Good mariner, hold fast to the helm, and if you can, try to escape. It is too late for some of you; it is too late for all of you! Into those rocks you must drive and perish, unless there shall come the ever-blessed Steersman of the Galilean lake, walking across the sea with pierced hands and feet, and bid the winds to hush and turn right round, and bid you believe in him, and then bid you steer to the port of glory, where all shall be rest and peace! God grant that such mercy may come to you! Pray for it, ask for it. Trust Jesus, and you shall have it, and to him shall be the praise, world without end. Amen.

A Memorable Milestone

"I have preached righteousness in the great congregation : lo, I have not refrained my lips, O Lord, thou knowest. I have not hid thy righteousness within my heart ; I have declared thy faithfulness and thy salvation : I have not concealed thy loving-kindness and thy truth from the great congregation. Withhold not thou thy tender mercies from me, O Lord : let thy lovingkindness and thy truth continually preserve me."—Ps. xl. 9—11.

SOMETIMES, dear friends, we should take a review of life. There are occasions when men feel bound to do so, and the retrospect may be full of profit to themselves. I find that many look back in hours of trouble. A dark cloud brings them to a pause. In prosperity they might have run on with very little thought, but sorrow calls them to a halt. They are driven to God in prayer, and at such times it is not unusual for them, if God has been gracious to them in the past, to recollect his great goodness, and to mention it while they are plead-ing at the mercy-seat. They say, "He hath dealt well with his servants. The Lord hath helped us hitherto." They look back, and see the Ebenezers which they have raised in past years, and then they cry, "Hath God forgotten to be gracious?"

> "And can he have taught me to trust in his name,
> And thus far have brought me to put me to shame?"

Thus they drive their griefs away, and the remembrance of past mercy helps them to snatch faggots from the altars of the bygone years, wherewith to kindle the sacrifice of the present moment.

Men are also accustomed to review their lives when they are brought near to the verge of the grave. It is helpful, when we fear that life is about to end, to begin to add it up, to see what the sum total reaches. If God should say to us, "Set thine house in order; for thou shalt die, and not live," the best way to do it is to remember the past, looking at what we have done, and what God has done; and then to set one against the other, that we may repent of

87

the sin, and may hope because of the mercy. Now, albeit that we may not ourselves be brought so near to death's door as that, yet during the past month or so we have, as a people, been continually going to the sepulchre. I think that there were seven notable brethren and sisters who fell asleep last week, so constantly have death's arrows been flying amongst us; therefore, as we are come to the margin of the river and are reminded that we must ourselves shortly put off this tabernacle, let us look back a little, and remember all the way the Lord our God has led us.

There are, however, other occasions apart from those of great sorrow or of apprehended departure, when wise men are fully warranted in considering the period as peculiarly noteworthy. I have come to such a time to-day. Twenty-five years have passed over our heads since I preached my first sermon in this house. The sanctuary was opened with songs of joy; many who were with us then are in glory now, and many of you who are with us to-day were not even born then. To those who were at the opening of the Tabernacle, it must seem almost an old building now. I hear people talk of "the dear old Tabernacle," and well they may, for a quarter of a century is no mean period in the history of a building or of a Church. There has been a great deal done in those twenty-five years, and we have, both personally and as a Church, enjoyed abounding mercy. I did not think it right to let the occasion pass over without offering devout thanksgiving to the Lord for all his lovingkindness to us, and endeavouring to say some words that shall perhaps make us feel more our indebtedness to God, and cause us to determine to be more than ever consecrated to his service.

This text, though it belongs first of all, in the divinest and fullest sense, to our gracious Master, belongs also to David, and through David to those whom God has called to bear testimony to the gospel of his grace. We can say, and we do say, humbly but most earnestly —and I know that there are many brethren here who can join us, each in his own ministry, and many brothers and sisters who, though not in the ministry, can say, at all event in the spirit of the words, after their measure—" I have preached righteousness in the great congregation : lo, I have not refrained my lips, O Lord, thou knowest. I have not hid thy righteousness within my heart; I have declared thy faithfulness and thy salvation : I have not concealed thy loving-kindness and thy truth from the great congregation."

I. Coming, then, to our text, here is, first, A CONTINUAL TESTIMONY. Many of you have borne testimony for God in your homes, as well as in your lives; some of you have borne the testimony in your classes in the Sunday-school; some in the streets; some in cottage meetings; some in larger assemblies. We, especially, who are called to the public ministry of the Word, have borne this testimony in " the great congregation." But all of us who are the Lord's servants have, I hope, borne our testimony according to our opportunities and abilities.

It has been imperfect, but it has been sincere. In looking back upon our testimony for God, we could almost wish to obliterate it because of its imperfections; but we can truthfully say that it has been sincerely borne up to the measure of the capacity given to us. It has been borne without a doubt, without any mental reservation, with intensity of spirit—borne because it could not be silenced. I have preached the gospel to you, my brethren and sisters, because I have believed it, and if what I have preached to you is not true I am a lost man. For me there is no joy in life and no hope in death except in that gospel which I have continually expounded here. It is not to me a theory. I would scarcely stop at saying that it is a belief. It has become matter of absolute fact to me. It is interwoven with my consciousness. It is part of my being. Every day makes it dearer to me; my joys bind me to it, my griefs drive me to it. All that is behind me, all that is before me, all that is above me, all that is beneath me, everything compels me to say that my testimony has been borne with my heart, and mind, and soul, and strength; and I am grateful to God that I can say this, putting it as the text puts it, "O Lord, thou knowest." If others do not know the truth of the matter, I rejoice that my Master knows my heart.

I feel grateful to God that I can say this because of *the subjects of the testimony.* The first subject of the psalmist's testimony had been God's "righteousness." That is the main point to be noticed in all testimony for God,—God's positive righteousness in himself; God's way of righteousness by which he justifies the ungodly; God's method of spreading righteousness in the world by the power and energy of his Holy Spirit. I, for one, believe in a God who punishes sin. I have never flattered you with the idea that sin is a trifle, and that in some future age it may expiate itself. Nay, the righteousness of God has seemed to me to be a dark background upon which to draw the bright lines of his everlasting love in Christ Jesus. In the expiation of Christ, the righteousness of God is vindicated to the full. He is "just, and the justifier of him that believeth in Jesus." I ask for no pardon to be given to me unrighteously. My conscience could not be satisfied with a forgiveness that came to me unjustly, for the glory of God would be dishonoured thereby. There would be a blot upon the heavenly statute-book if sin were pardoned without atonement. But we have preached the righteousness of God; and we feel that, in doing so, we lay a sure foundation, upon which to build the comfort and hope of the believer in Christ Jesus.

In addition to the righteousness of God, the psalmist had preached his "faithfulness." The Lord keeps all his promises. He is the Faithful Promiser, what he promises he performs. There is no lie in him, nor change, nor shadow of a turning. "Hath he said, and shall he not do?" Which of his promises ever failed? Has he drawn back even in the least degree from his covenant, or altered the word which has gone forth out of his lips? Our testimony has not been borne to a fickle God, and a feeble salvation, which saves for a time, and after all does not really save, but suffers saints to fall away, and perish everlastingly. Nay, we have given unfaltering utterance to that declaration of our Lord, "I give unto my sheep eternal life; and they shall never perish, neither shall any pluck them out of my hand." We believe in everlasting love, in an everlasting covenant, ordered in all things and sure; and therefore righteousness and faithfulness have been the two foundations of our ministry, upon which we have tried to build a gospel worth our preaching and worth your having.

Then the psalmist says that he had borne testimony to two things in conjunction with each other: " Thy lovingkindness and thy truth." Oh, brothers and sisters, what a theme is here! " Thy lovingkindness!" God's generous mercy, his overflowing love, his kinned-ness, his kindness, to his chosen, whom he has made to be a people near unto himself, to whom he manifests his very soul. That word " loving," added to the word " kindness," makes it a gem doubly precious. Where is there among words any other equal to this,—" lovingkindness"? I have exulted to preach to you the lovingkindness of the Lord. I needed not to be driven to this happy task. I have almost needed sometimes to be stopped when I have passed the hour, and my theme has carried me away. Oh, the lovingkindness of the Lord to those that put their trust under the shadow of his wings! That is a subject on which one might preach for ever, and yet not exhaust its treasures.

And then his " truth "—God's truth; the truth of his Word; the truth of his Son; the truth of the great doctrines which are given to us in the gospel. I have not preached to you any sort of speculation. I have never sought to invent new forms of truth. It shall be seen one day whose thoughts shall stand, God's thoughts or man's; and it shall be seen which is the true ministry, that which takes up God's Word, and echoes it, or that which boils it down until the very life is extracted from it. I have no sympathy with the preaching which degrades God's truth into a hobby-horse for its own thought, and only looks upon Scripture as a kind of pulpit from which it may thunder out its own opinions. Nay, if I have gone beyond what that Book has taught, may God blot out everything that I have said! I beseech you, never believe me if I go an atom beyond what is plainly taught there. I am content to live and to die as the mere repeater of Scriptural teaching; as a person who has thought out nothing, and invented nothing; as one who never thought invention to be any part of his calling; but who concluded that he was to take the message from the lips of God to the best of his ability, and simply to be a mouth for God to the people, mourning much that anything of his own should come between, but never thinking that he was somehow to refine the message or to adapt it to the brilliance of this wonderful century, and then to hand it out as being so much his own that he might take some share of the glory of it. Nay, nay; we have aimed at nothing of the kind. " I have declared *thy* faithfulness and *thy* salvation: I have not concealed *thy* lovingkindness and *thy* truth from the great congregation." Nothing have we preached as our own. If there has been anything of our own, we do bitterly take back those words, and eat them, and repent that ever we should have been guilty of the sin and folly of uttering them. The things which we have learned of God our Father, and of his Son Jesus Christ, by his Holy Spirit, we have sought to speak unto you.

Now, dear friends, let me say, next, that this text describes *a work which has been done under great difficulties.* It may seem a very easy thing simply to have a message and to tell it. Yes, it appears so; but it is not so easy as it looks at first sight. I do not suppose that you always find your servants deliver your messages accurately. Did you ever sit round a table, and tell one person a story, and ask him to tell it to his neighbour? Let each one whisper it; and by the time it gets to the end of the table you will scarcely recognize your tale; it will have been altered so much. There is a tendency in the minds of all of us to alter what we tell, and it is a struggle to keep to the exact truth. Besides, this is an age which likes pretty things, —something fresh and new; and it is not easy always to swim up-stream, and to go against the tendency of the time, and the spirit of the age. We have no particular desire to be thought fools any more than anybody else; and we know where all the wisdom is; at least, we ought to know, for we hear often enough about it. Ask the brethren of the "modern thought" school if they have not all the wisdom that is to be had nowadays. If they do not say that they have, many of them act as if they thought they had. No, friends, it is not so easy, after all, just to keep to the plain truth. There is a brother who has struck out something wonderfully fresh. We read his book; shall we not at least go with him a little way? You will find, brethren, that if you determine to hold fast the faith once for all delivered to the saints, you will have a battle to fight, in which you will be beaten unless you rely upon God for strength. If you are willing to let truth go, you have but to seek to please man, and it is soon done; and then you will be greeted with, "Hail fellow! Well met." But if you mean to declare God's truth, you will need the help of the Most High in the struggle.

But, although this testimony has been borne under difficulties, *it has been attended with unutterable pleasure.* Oh, the delight of preaching the gospel! I often say to young men who apply for admission to the College, "Do not become a minister if you can help it." But if you cannot help it, if a divine destiny drives you on, thank God that it is so! You are a happier man, if you are able to preach the gospel, than if you had been elected to a throne. There is no business like it under heaven. I have heard some say that our professional study of the Word of God may be a hindrance to our growth in the divine life. I know what they mean, and there is some truth in their words; but to me, the preaching of the gospel has been a continual means of grace, and I can say with the Apostle Paul, "Unto me, who am less than the least of all saints, is this *grace* given, that I should preach among the Gentiles the unsearchable riches of Christ." It really is a grace to be permitted to preach the gospel; it brings grace with it. Brethren in the ministry, have you not read the Bible much more because you have had to preach the blessed truths revealed in it? Have you not been driven to your knees much more because you have had to deal with anxious souls, and to lead the people of God? I am sure that it is so; and I thank God for giving me a calling which does not take me away from the mercy-seat, but drives me to it. I am grateful that I have a message which I am glad to tell, glad to tell anywhere, a message which never needs to be concealed, but which brings joy to us in telling it, and salvation to our hearers in listening to it. Blessed be God that we have such a story to proclaim!

I could say much more about this first point, but I must not, for our time is so short. This must suffice upon the subject of our continual testimony.

II. Now, secondly, the text mentions A REMARKABLE AUDIENCE. The psalmist says, twice over, " I have preached righteousness in *the great congregation ;*" and yet again, " I have not concealed thy loving-kindness and thy truth from *the great congregation.*"

It is *astonishing to the preacher* that there should be a great congregation to hear the gospel. I do not know how you think of it, but if anybody had been set here to speak so many times a week upon politics, I wonder whether he would have had a crowded congregation at the end of twenty-five years. My friend Mr. Varley speaks right mightily; but if he had been preaching upon total abstinence for twenty-five years, I am sure that some would have totally abstained from coming to hear him. If I had had to preach here upon—well, what topic shall I say?—the object that the Liberation Society has in view, for instance, I am afraid that I should have liberated many of you from attendance long before this. All other subjects are exhaustible; but give us that Book, and give us the Holy Ghost, and we may preach on for ever. We shall never get to the end of it. I have heard of two infidels, one of whom said to his fellow, " If you had to go to jail for twelve months, and you could only have one book, what book would you choose? " He was very surprised when his companion said, " Oh, I should take the Bible! " The first one said, " But you do not believe in it; I wonder that you should choose that." " Oh! but," rejoined his friend, " it is no end of a book." His record is true, it is " no end of a book." Jerome used to say, "I adore the infinity of Holy Scripture;" and well he might. I would like you to look at my Bible at home, which is marked with all the texts I have preached from. There are thirty-one completed volumes of my sermons; and the thirty-second is in the making.* Of course, in addition to the thirty-two volumes in the regular weekly series, there are many more volumes printed, and I have all the texts marked from which I have preached. I sometimes make the outline of a sermon, and then, when I turn to my Bible, I find that I have preached from that text, and the sermon has been published, and I say, " That will not do for a Sunday morning." I do not want to have the same subject again oftener than I can help. Sometimes, however, I find that the same text may be taken, and a new sermon readily enough made from it, for there is a springing well in Holy Scripture, never exhausted, and the great congregation wants continually to come to hear repetitions of the same great truth, though it is ever the preacher's duty to seek for acceptable words in presenting it. Young

---

* This discourse begins the fifty-first volume of Spurgeon's Sermons. How little the preacher thought, when he praised God for twenty-five years' ministry in the Metropolitan Tabernacle, that he should continue to declare God's faithfulness and salvation week by week to the great company of Sermon readers for so many years after he had put off the tabernacle of the body.

man, just beginning to preach, do not be afraid to stick to your texts; that is the best way to get variety in your discourses. Saturate your sermons with Bibline, the essence of Bible truth, and you will always have something new to say.

But when I think of the great congregation, *how encouraging it is!* It is always good fishing where there are plenty of fish. We are bound to go and angle for a single soul, wherever there is one to be found, and some do great service for the Master who take the fish one by one. But what a delight it is to have the great seine net of the gospel, and throw it into such a lake as this, God guiding the hand of the fisherman the while! Surely he should be a happy man!

But then, dear friends, when we think of this great congregation, *what solemn thoughts come over our mind!* I come down to this platform sometimes, and when I get another look at this great congregation, I am staggered. Time after time I have felt as if I could run away sooner than face this tremendous throng again, and speak to them once more. O sirs, to think of all these being dying men and dying women, and to think that this gospel that I preach is needed by them all, and may be refused by many with awful consequences, and may be accepted by some (it will be, thank God) with consequences of unutterable joy! To think that we shall have to give an account of how we have preached, and how you have heard! To think that we shall all meet again at the judgment-seat, to give an account of every Sunday and every Thursday service! If Xerxes could not restrain a tear at the thought of his myriads of men passing away, who can look at congregations like this without being moved with compassion? Yes, yes; it is not easy to preach to a great congregation so as to be able to say at the last, " I am pure from the blood of all men, for I have not shunned to declare unto you all the counsel of God."

The sight of this great congregation gathered to-night *suggests many memories.* I recollect some dear ones that used to sit here, and there, and there, and there. I can almost see them now; some dear old saints with grey heads, that used to be our glory, who are now with God; some young and ardent spirits, that were taken away before they reached their prime. You sit where sat some who loved your Master well, and served him faithfully. Worthily occupy their places, beloved friends.

But excuse me if I say no more upon this topic. My brain seems in a whirl, as dissolving views pass before my memory in quick succession. If you want to see life and death, stand here. I feel like the captain of a vessel on the bridge. I am looking down on you who are the passengers and crew; but yet, from another point of view, I seem to be looking at great waves that sweep by, and more come, and others follow; ever a succession of changes, nothing abiding. How long shall we remain? How soon shall we, too, also go? Well, it is something to have preached Christ to this great congregation. It is something to believe that those who have not received him are without excuse. It is much better to believe that many have received him, and that we shall meet them in the glory-land, rejoicing in that glorious sacrifice by which they have been cleansed from sin, in that dear Saviour by whose life and death they have been quickened, and made heirs of eternal glory. Oh, that this faith may be in us all, and that we may all at last join in the general assembly of the Church of the Firstborn, whose names are written in heaven!

III. I have only a few minutes left, in which to expatiate upon the last of the three points, THE SUGGESTED PRAYER. May I just give you an outline of what I would have said if we could have spared more time? The prayer of the psalmist is,—" Withhold not thou thy tender mercies from me, O Lord : let thy lovingkindness and thy truth "—the things which he had preached—" continually preserve me."

This prayer is *suitable for the preacher*, and he prays it now. Taking David's words, and making them my own, I pray to the Lord at this moment,—" Withhold not thou thy tender mercies from *me*, O Lord : let thy lovingkindness and thy truth continually preserve *me*."

The prayer is also *suitable for every Christian here*. Let me read it, and let every Christian pray it now : " Withhold not thou thy tender mercies from *me*, O Lord : let thy lovingkindness and thy truth continually preserve *me*."

With a little alteration, *this prayer may suit you who are not yet saved*, but who desire to be : " Withhold not thou thy tender mercies from *me*, O Lord." Are you praying it? Is not this a good time in which to pray that prayer? The signs are all propitious. There is " the sound of a going in the tops of the mulberry-trees." There are tokens for good abroad. There is dew about to-night. Now, therefore, pray this prayer if thou hast never prayed before ; and God help thee to claim the answer by appropriating faith!

It seems to me that this prayer was suggested to the psalmist by at least three things.

First, *it was suggested by the great congregation*. David seems to say, " O Lord, there are so many others who need thy care, let me not be lost in the crowd, withhold not thy tender mercies from me."

> " Lord, I hear of showers of blessing
> Thou art scattering, full and free ;
> Showers, the thirsty land refreshing ;
> Let some droppings fall on me,
>   Even me."

Next, *the subject suggested it*. " Thy truth, thy lovingkindness, O Lord ; let these preserve me. I hear of thy goodness ; I cannot bear to miss it. I hear of thy truth ; I would not be a stranger to it. Lord, bless me, even me! "

Then, again, *the future suggested it*. The psalmist expected to suffer great trials and serious afflictions, and therefore he prayed, " Let thy lovingkindness and thy truth continually preserve me."

Now, as a congregation, we have completed twenty-five years in this building ; but we must not reckon that we have reached the end of our struggles, or even the end of our sins. O brothers and sisters, this is only a part of the way to heaven. I think that I told you, once before, that some friends, when they raise an Ebenezer, sit down on the top of it, and say, " Here we are going to stop." When this Tabernacle was opened, I remember that that night I put a sharp iron spike on the top of "the stone of help," that nobody might sit upon it; and I do the same again on the Ebenezer stone I now raise in remembrance of God's goodness. Let none of us sit down at the end of this twenty-fifth year, and say, "We have come so far, and here we are going to stay." Long nights of darkness lie beyond, there are giants to be fought, mountains to be climbed, rivers to be crossed. Who dreams of ease, while he is here in the enemy's country? Out with your sword, man! You have not done with the battle. Awake, thou that sleepest! Thou hast not come yet to the place of resting. This is the place for watching, and praying, and wrestling, and struggling. Therefore do we cry, "Withhold not thou thy tender mercies from me." We are getting older; we are getting weaker; we are, perhaps, getting less wise. . Who knows that all our years will bring us good news? They may bring us evil if we trust to our past experience. We want God with us now as much as ever we did. Therefore let us cry to him, "From this night do thou bless us more and more."

The poor psalmist was in great trouble when he prayed this prayer. He says, "Innumerable evils have compassed me about." Therefore he says, "Withhold not thou thy tender mercies from me."

He adds, "Mine iniquities have taken hold upon me." If there is one here whose conscience is accusing him, and who is guilty before his God, let him pray this prayer because of his iniquities.

He goes on to say, "I am not able to look up." If that is your case, if you cannot look up, pray the Lord to look down, and cry to him never to take his mercy from you.

David further says, concerning his iniquities, "They are more than the hairs of my head : therefore my heart faileth me." Well, when our heart does fail us, let us recollect the mercy which has helped us so long, and let us cast ourselves again upon that mercy for all that lies before us.

I am not going to venture upon any prophecy. I attended, on Wednesday, the funeral of our beloved brother Dr. Stanford. You may attend mine before this year is over; or I may attend yours. If you could draw up the curtain that hides the future, you would not wish to do it, would you? Trust the Lord so that, if you live, you are prepared to live; and if you die, you are prepared to die. I think that the best thing you can do is to do the next thing that comes to you, and to do it thoroughly well. I was here last Monday. I had no rest from spiritual work from three in the afternoon till half-past nine at night; and about the middle of it I felt, "Well, I do not know how I shall get through this long, long afternoon of seeing enquirers and candidates for Church-fellowship." So I said to a brother, "How am I to do it all?" However, there was a cup of tea in front of me, and I said, "I think I will drink that tea; that is the next thing to be done." Oftentimes that will be your best course, just do the next thing you can do when you are saying to yourself, "How shall I do if I live to be old?" When you go home to-night, eat your supper, and go to bed to the glory of God ; and when you get up in the morning, do not think about what you are going to do at night. Do what comes to you when you begin the day's work, and keep right straight on. If you can see a step at a time, that is about as far as you need to see. Do not begin prying into the future; but just go straight on from day to day, depending on God for the mercy and grace and strength of the day. That is the way to live, and I am persuaded that is the way to die. Mr. Wesley said, "If I knew that I was to die to-night, and I had an engagement to attend a class-meeting, I should go to it. If I had promised to call and see old Betty So-and-so on the way back, I should call in to see her. I have then to go home, and have family prayer. I would do that. Then I should take my boots off, and I should go to bed, just as I should do if I were not going to die." Oh, do not let death be a sort of addition to the programme, which was not calculated upon; but so live that whenever it comes—if it come while we are sitting here to-night—you will be ready for it. Then yours will be a happy life, a joyful life, a useful life. Secularism teaches us that we ought to look to this world. Christianity teaches us that the best way to prepare for this world is to be fully prepared for the next. Why, it elevates and glorifies the secular duties, which else would trail in the mire, if our conversation, our citizenship, is in heaven, even while we are on the earth. God bless you, beloved! Let us praise his name for all the mercies of the past quarter of a century, and trust his grace for all the future.

Reasons

for Doubting Christ

"Wherefore didst thou doubt?"—Matthew xiv. 31.

OUR LORD did not begin his dealings with Peter on this emergency by asking him that question. He first stretched out his hand and saved him from his peril, and then he said to him, "O thou of little faith, wherefore didst thou doubt?" When a man is in trouble, help him out first, and then blame him for having got into it, if you feel it necessary to do so. It is cruel to bring your censure to bear upon sinking Peter. First give him your help, lest he perish in the sea, and when you have done that you may afterwards chide him for any fault that you perceive in him. This is always the way with our Master. He giveth liberally and upbraideth not, except when there shall come to be a special reason for our spiritual profit, when a little upbraiding may do us good.

Now I am going, first, to use our text, and then I am going to alter it. I shall first speak to God's people, and say, "Wherefore didst thou doubt, O Christian?" and then put it into another tense altogether, and address it to the unconverted, and say, "Wherefore *dost* thou doubt, O thou who knowest the gospel, but hast not yet believed it?"

I. LET US USE THE TEXT, AND QUESTION GOD'S PEOPLE : "Wherefore didst thou doubt?" I am probably addressing some brothers and sisters—perhaps a great many who have been through a season of profound gloom, and in the midst of that gloom there has been the element of spiritual evil. To be gloomy and depressed is not sinful at all, but there may have been in the midst of that the sin of unbelief : there may have been a doubting of God—a distrust of his providence —a questioning of his love. Now I come at this time to such a brother or sister, and say, "O thou of little faith, wherefore didst thou doubt?" Can you answer that question? Shall I help you?

First, I will suppose some reasons which, if they do exist, will justify you in having doubted ; and then I will take the reasons

97

you yourselves assign one by one. I shall put them to you to know whether the supposition is allowable.

You may doubt *if on former occasions you have found God unfaithful to his promise.* If he has lied unto you,—if, after having said, "I will never leave thee nor forsake thee," you have found, say on one occasion at the least, that he has utterly failed you and forsaken you, then you are perfectly justified in doubting him for the future, and you were justified in doubting him just now. What say you to the supposition? I would not ask you to speak what is not true, even for God himself, for there is nothing more detestable in God's sight than for us to attempt to honour him by falsehood. A pious fraud is a most impious blasphemy. No, speak the truth. Has the Lord been a wilderness or a land of darkness to you? Has he said, and has he not done it? Can you put your finger upon a single promise, and say, "I relied upon this, and I found it failed me? He said that they that trusted in him should never be ashamed nor confounded?" Can you say that you did trust him in some particular event, and the failure you experienced made you to be ashamed? Brothers and sisters, I know what you will say to that supposition. You are grieved almost to hear it made. You rise up with loving indignation, and you say, "God is faithful and true. He has not gone back from his promise in any single instance." Then, brother, very softly will I put it—and I have reasons for doing it very softly—O thou of little faith, if it be so, wherefore didst thou doubt? If he helped thee before, why didst thou doubt him in the next trouble? If he fed the five thousand with the loaves and the fishes, why didst thou think that he could not make thee also walk the waters of the sea?

There is another supposition : you may doubt *if your case is a new one, and so superlatively difficult that it is quite certain that God cannot help you in it.* You require something more than omnipotence; and the case is so perplexing that even omniscience cannot see a way out of it. Now, as I make that supposition, my heart is laughing at the very absurdity of the terms I use, for if we say *omni-potence*, that is all power. It is not possible that anything should be beyond that. And if we say *omni-science*, that is all wisdom. It is not even imaginable that anything can surpass that; so I think I had better dismiss this supposition at once. Only it is sometimes put in Scripture by way of question, "Is anything too hard for the Lord?" "The Lord's hand is not shortened that it cannot save, neither his ear heavy that it cannot hear?" When you answer, "I know that God is able, and I know that God is wise to help me," then I must whisper that question again, "O thou of little faith, wherefore didst thou doubt?"

But I will suppose something else, that you may doubt *if God has abolished the promises.* Dear brother, is it true that the Bible has run out and become like an old almanac that is done with,—that God has spoken somewhere in the dark places of the earth, and has said that the seed of Jacob may seek his face in vain, and that he will not be held to his covenant or bound to a single promise that he has made—that he has revoked them all. You are astonished that I should even utter such a supposition. Your soul rises indignantly to repel the imagination, for if you say, " All the promises of God in him are yea, and in him amen unto the Glory of God by us." You know, and you are assured, that he cannot change. He is " the same yesterday, to-day, and for ever," and you are quite certain that he speaks the truth when he says, " my covenant will I not break, nor alter the thing that has gone out of my lips." " God is not a man that he should lie, neither the son of man that he should repent." You are persuaded of all this, my dear brother, are you not? Then, all those promises being true, and all confirmed with the sprinkled blood of Christ, I must have your ear yet again while I just whisper into it, " Wherefore, then, didst thou doubt? Wherefore didst thou doubt? "

There is only one more supposition, but it is the worst of all. You may doubt, *if God himself has entirely changed*—a supposition which has been put by the psalmist in other language, " Will he be favourable no more? Is his mercy clean gone for ever? Doth his promise fail for evermore? Hath God forgotten to be gracious? Hath he in anger shut up his tender mercies? " Now, do you believe for a single moment that God is changed in his love or in the objects of it? Do you think that he has cast away his people whom he did foreknow? that Christ will lose that which he bought with his precious blood? that he will strike off the precious stones of his breastplate the names which from eternity were written there? that he will forget the children of his choice when he said, " Can a woman forget her sucking child, that she should not have compassion on the son of her womb? yea, they may forget, yet will I not forget thee "? And, again, " the mountains shall depart and the hills be removed, but my kindness shall not depart from thee, neither the covenant of. my peace be removed, saith the Lord that hath mercy on thee "? And yet again, " I am God; I change not; therefore ye sons of Jacob are not consumed "? Do you not remember reading the words, " Having loved his own which were in the world, he loved them unto the end "? Well, brothers, since those things are so, I shall have to come back to my old question, and say, " O·thou of little faith, with an unchanged God to trust to, wherefore didst thou doubt? "

Now, I cannot think of any other supposition that might make it justifiable to doubt, so now I am going to hear—or I will repeat on your behalf—some of the answers to the question which, perhaps, you would give.

First, I hear one say, " I doubted *because my sinful life became unusually clear and distinct to me*. I hope I have been converted, have felt my need of Christ, and have put my trust in him. But I never had such a sight of myself as I had a little while ago. It seemed as if the fountains of the great deep were broken up; I saw that I had sinned foully and fallen far; my best actions I discovered to be polluted, and the whole of my life to be marred through and through with an evil spirit and with everything that was contrary to the mind of God; when I saw sin like that, then it was that I doubted." Yes, dear brother, I know your feelings, and such doubts as yours often—too often—come upon men. But did you not know, was it not told you from the beginning, that your sin was such that you were condemned in the sight of God, and accursed by the law? Did you not know that in spite of your sin "Christ Jesus came into the world to save sinners," even the very chief? Did not you know God willed not the death of any sinner, and that "the blood of Jesus Christ his Son cleanseth us from all sin"? Yes, you did know it; and therefore I can only dismiss that excuse by saying that since thou didst know that, with all thy sin, the boundless atonement was able to meet it,—since thou didst know that, with all thy blackness, the fountain filled with blood had power to wash it out, "O thou of little faith wherefore didst thou doubt?"

"Ah," say you, "but it was not quite a sight of my past sin: it was *because of my sinfulness by nature*. I thought after I was converted that I should not feel any sin within me, or that, if I did know its presence by experience that I should conquer it; instead of that it has been a fight with me every day, and only the other day, when I was exposed to temptation, I was carried right off my feet; when I got alone into my chamber, and saw how badly I had acted, I looked into my heart, and discovered it to be still full of all manner of evil; and, though I hope there is some grace within me, yet is there so much of the old nature that I know not what to do. That is why I doubt." Yes, but, my dear brother or sister, whichever you may be, did not you know of old that the Lord Jesus Christ came to destroy the works of the devil in you, and that where he has begun the good work he will carry it on? Did not you know that the Spirit of God is given to help our infirmities, and that he sanctifieth us and all the elect people of God,—that from day to day he leads us to the fountain for sin and for uncleanness in order to be cleansed from sin, and that he brings us the power to overcome sin? Did not you know that Christ is able to keep you from falling, and to present you faultless before his presence with exceeding joy? Yes, you did know that; and therefore that meets all difficulty, and I have to say to you again that the excuse will not hold water. "O thou of little faith, wherefore didst thou doubt?"

"Ah, sir," says one, "you do not know everything. I doubted *because I have been in a case such as never happened to anybody before*. I was in a dreadful trouble. O sir, my trouble was so peculiar that I could not tell it to anybody, and I should not have liked to have done so. Wave after wave swept over me. I could not see any way of escape from it at all. It was so extraordinary that I am sure that I must be *the* man that hath seen affliction, peculiarly marked out from all the rest." Yes, dear friend, that is very likely. I know a great many that have entertained the same opinion of themselves that you do of yourself, and I have sometimes put myself down in the category though you may not think so; but do not you know that it is said, "Many are the afflictions of the righteous, but the Lord delivereth him out of them all"? Did you never read, "In the world ye shall have tribulation, but be of good cheer, I have overcome the world"? Did you never hear of Gad, of whom it is said that, "a troop shall overcome him, but he shall overcome at the last"? Have you not read, "They shall surely gather together against thee, but not by me. Whosoever shall gather together against thee shalt fall for thy sake. No weapon that is formed against thee shall prosper, and every tongue that shall rise against thee in judgment thou shalt condemn." Did you not know that? If you did not, there was the book which you might have searched to find the promise. And, knowing all that, dear friend, though thy case may be peculiar, thou shouldest not have given place to doubt at all, for thou hast a unique Saviour. His people are a peculiar people, but he is a peculiarly glorious Deliverer and Captain to them, and he will bring all of them safely to the eternal glory. Therefore, "O thou of little faith, wherefore didst thou doubt?"

I can suppose another person answering on quite another score. He says, "Ah, sir, I doubted in anticipation of the trouble *because I felt I could not bear the trial.* I felt that I should sink under it, if it did happen. O sir, I had a fear upon me that if it did occur I should perish." Yes, I know that experience too. How did it turn out? Did the dreaded ill occur? "No," say you. Then why did you want to be crossing the bridge before you came to it? "Oh, but it did occur," say you. Have you perished by it then, brother? "No," you are compelled to answer; "I found such strange assistance given in the time of need, and such singular succours just when I was in my deepest temptation. You know, sir, I had looked for the trouble, but I never expected to find such friends as God raised up, and such remarkable helps as he found for me." Ah, I see, God has given you two eyes, and you shut up one of them. You had only looked at the dark side, but you did not look at the bright side. "Oh, but," perhaps you say, "I did not think there was any bright side." No, I know you did not, but God knew that it was there; has not he said to you of old many times, "Cast thy burden on the Lord and he will sustain thee"? That is to say, whether there is a bright side to it or not, cast it on the Lord and it will be well with you. "He shall never suffer the righteous to be moved." "Trust in the Lord and do good: so shalt thou dwell in the land, and verily thou shalt be fed." You may say, in confidence, "When my father and my mother forsake me, then the Lord will take me up," for he has said, "I will never fail thee nor forsake thee." Well, you knew of this, and so I come back to my question, "O thou of little faith, wherefore didst thou doubt?"

I could multiply these cases, but I ask each friend who has been doubting to state his own reason to his own heart: he will easily be able to find an answer also.

Now, I want your ear just a minute or two in order to see how your doubts and fears look under certain aspects. "Wherefore didst thou doubt?"

Look at your doubts in the light of your conversion. You remember when first you knew the Lord. You remember those happy days and weeks when you were first converted, it was the time of your spiritual honeymoon. Suppose, at those times, somebody had said to you, "You will doubt the Saviour." You would have said, "Never! Why, the wonders of

God's grace to me in saving such a lost wretch as I am are so extraordinary that others may doubt, but I never shall." • Well, then, just look at these doubts in that light.

After that you had a severe trial, but now you have got out of the difficulty which troubled you, have you not? You have gained the shore again after your buffeting with the waves. Now, I want you to *look at your doubts in the light of your deliverance.* The preacher need scarcely tell how disgusted he has been with himself, when he has passed through a trial, to think that he could not have left it in the hands of God, but he began tinkering the matter himself and made a failure of it because he tried to meet the need with his own wisdom, which was nothing but perfect folly and ignorance. Do you not feel the same? Could not you set yourself up for a scarecrow, and laugh at yourself? I am sure you could if the Lord has delivered you.

Once more. *How do you feel about your doubts when you get into Jesus Christ's bosom,*—when your head is where the head of John was, and the Lord is looking at you, and saying, "I have loved thee with an everlasting love." Suppose the next thing he said was, "Wherefore didst thou doubt?" Why, you would look at him with the tears in your eyes, and say, "Dear Master, I pray you do not say anything about it, I am so ashamed of my doubt. Oh, let it be forgotten. • I never had any cause to distrust thee. I grieve to think that I should ever have got into a state where such doubts were possible."

I will put you in another position. *How do you feel about your doubts when you try to teach other people?* Here is a dear, doubting sister, or brother, and you are trying to comfort the downcast soul. How do you think about yourself when you wanted comfort yourself, when you were down in that very way? It is a dreadful thing for a man, when he is very sad and low-spirited, if some Christian brother goes and cuts a bit out of the man's own sermons, and sends it to him. I have had that experience myself sometimes, and, as I have read my own words, I have said, "What a fool I am!" That is wonderfully near the truth when you say it about yourself brother. I do not think we have ever hit the nail on the head much more clearly than when we say we are foolish and ignorant—for that is exactly what we are, only with a dash of sin with the folly, when we begin to doubt the ever blessed God, who ought to be trusted with very implicit confidence, even as a little child trusts to its mother's love. Never ought a doubt to come into our hearts towards our Saviour.

And *how do you think your doubts will look when you get to heaven and look back at them?* Mrs. Hannah More tells us that she went into a carpet factory, and when she looked at the carpet she could not make out any design, and she thought that there had been some mistake. There were long pieces that seemed to have no beauty in them whatever; but the manufacturer said, "Madam, I will take you round to the other side"; then she saw the beauty of the pattern that was being woven into the fabric. Well, now, while you and I are here, we are full of doubts, because we cannot make the pattern out. We are the wrong side of the carpet; but when we get to heaven, and see all that God intended and worked for us, I think that even in heaven we shall call ourselves fools, and say, "How could I have judged before my time that splendid design of providence which was hidden in the infinite wisdom and love of God's gracious heart? How could I have been dissatisfied with that which was working my lasting good?" Wherefore, then, didst thou doubt?

Two or three words just to say that I think that I can give the reason why some Christians do doubt occasionally. Perhaps their brain is weary. I pity them; but they must not pity themselves too much. Perhaps they have not been living near to God. Perhaps they were getting rather proud, and thought that if they walked on the water they must be fine fellows. Perhaps they took their eye off their Master; I reckon that was what Peter did; he began to look at the winds and the waves, and therefore he could not be looking at Christ too. Perhaps they began to walk by sight, instead of by faith, and that is enough to make anybody sink. Some cause or other there must have been; but, whatever cause it' was, it is cause for sorrow, cause for regret, cause for repentance, for the Lord deserves to be implicitly trusted. In answer to his question, "Wherefore didst thou doubt?" we give this reply, "Good Lord, forgive thy servants in this thing, and lead us in quietness and patience to possess our souls."

Thus much to the people of God.

II. Now, LET US SLIGHTLY ALTER THE TEXT AND QUESTION THOSE THAT ARE NOT GOD'S PEOPLE. We will pause a minute, and use the text in another tense. The Lord Jesus Christ has been into this world and done a great deal for sinners; and, as the result of what he has done, he has bidden us go and proclaim everywhere free salvation through his precious blood; he declares that whosoever believeth in him shall not perish, but shall have everlasting life. Many know all about this. They are well acquainted with the truth of substitution, and the way in which God can be just and yet the justifier of the ungodly; but they are still full of doubts. They have not believed. Dear friend, I think I can give you some good reasons for your doubting, if I am allowed a little scope for imagination.

And I suppose, first of all, that *you have heard of a number of others that have been to Christ and have believed in him, and yet have perished.* If you have really known such persons, you are perfectly justified in not believing in Christ. You have a brother, I suppose, that trusted Christ and yet died in despair. You have a sister, perhaps, that put all her confidence in the Lord Jesus Christ, and yet was not saved. Now, I am absolutely certain that nothing of the kind has ever occurred. I am equally certain that beneath the copes of heaven, during all time since Adam fell, there has never been a solitary instance of a soul sincerely seeking the mercy of God through Jesus Christ, and putting its trust in him, and yet missing eternal salvation. So if you cannot have that reason why do you continue to doubt?

I will suppose another reason, namely, that *you yourself have been to God with earnest prayer, seeking salvation and trusting in Jesus, and yet you have been refused.* Now, I am sure that that is not so —absolutely sure. I remember the instance of a man who did not even believe in God, or, at least, he thought he did not, but he was aroused to a sense of his danger, and he went to God with some such prayer as this: " O God," he said, " if there be a God, convince me of thy being. Lead me to thyself, if it be that I have sinned against thee, and thou art angry with me; and I fear it is so. And if thou hast sent thy Son to be an atonement for sin, let me know the power of that atonement." He said that that was all he dared to say at first; but he ended in solid faith and in a renewed heart and life. No matter how far off a man may be from God, if there be a hearty and earnest seeking after him through Jesus Christ, he must find him. You have not tried it: I am sure you have not tried it. If you had done so you must have succeeded. Were it possible that a man had tried simple trust in Christ, and were not saved, then, indeed, he might give a reason why he doubts. But you have no such reason.

I cannot think of any other, except that *you have been informed that the blood of Jesus Christ has lost its power.* Have you been assured that the gospel is abrogated? Have you been given to understand that the New Testament is a dead letter? Have you been persuaded that the gates of mercy are shut? Have you been led to believe that the invitations of grace are no more to be given? " Oh, no," say you; " our state were wretched indeed, if that were the case." Well, then, brother, as long as there is blood in the fountain, wherefore dost thou doubt its power to cleanse thee? As long as there is good news for sinners, why dost thou write bitter things against thyself? As long as a promise stands, and there is the invitation, " Whosoever will, let him take the water of life freely," wherefore dost thou doubt? Surely, if these things be as the book declares—that the Lord is ready to have mercy upon the very chief of sinners, who come and put their trust in Jesus Christ— you have no cause whatever to start back.

Well, now, I am inclined here to quit your reasons, as I cannot suppose any others that are not conspicuously false. But I can imagine that you suppose that *you have such great and special sins that you cannot think Christ can save you.* Now, I undertake to say this from a very wide experience and observation of persons converted to God,—that if you will mention any sin that you have committed, I will mention someone who fell into that same sin, and who has been saved from it; if you mention the peculiar aggravations connected with your life, I think that even my own observation will enable me to mention some person who, if not exactly in that form, yet, in some other equally bad, has gone as far into sin as you have done, and yet has been saved, who, though guilty of crimes unmentionable, has yet been washed in the blood of the Lamb and made whiter than snow. O beloved, we cannot be telling you always of what we know, but we do sometimes delight to think that there are cases in holy Scripture which we may tell of as much as we like. There is cruel, savage Manasseh; there is blood-thirsty, -threatening-breathing Saul; there is the woman that was a sinner; and there is the dying thief that rejoiced to find cleansing in the wounds of Christ. And why should not you be forgiven? There is no cause for doubt.

"But my point," says one, "is, Can this be for me?" *You believe the Gospel is true, but you doubt whether it is for you.* Well, no; it is not for you, if you are not a sinner. If thou canst say, "I am not guilty," then farewell to all hope, for Jesus Christ came into the world to save sinners. If you are a sinner, surely he came to save such as you are. The blessings of the gospel covenant are directed to the lost. "The Son of man is come to seek and to save that which was lost." Can you not get in there? Perhaps you remember Mr. Whitfield's speech to his brother, who had long been in distress of mind, who said at last, across the table, "George, I am lost." George said, "I am glad to hear it," and answering his brother's startled expression, he continued, "because the Son of man is come to seek and to save that which was lost." That brief utterance of the gospel lifted his brother out of despair into a clear and abiding hope in Jesus Christ. Perhaps you have heard of Mr. Whitfield again, in the Countess of Huntingdon's house, when some great lord complained to her ladyship that Mr. Whitfield had used most extraordinary language in his last sermon, most repulsive to men of taste. Mr. Whitfield said he was there to answer for himself, and he asked what the expression was that he had used. "Why," said the nobleman, "you said that Jesus Christ was willing to receive the devil's castaways." "Yes," he said, "I did say that, and I mean to say it again. Did your ladyship observe that I was called out of the room a few minutes ago because the bell rang?" "Yes," said the Countess. "And when I went to the door," continued Mr. Whitfield, "a poor creature stood there who had been living in a state of sin, and had come to such a condition that even those that associated with her before were unwilling to come near her. She had become unfit even for the lowest work to which the devil himself could put her, and she found her old companions had cast her away. She heard me preach in Tottenham Court, and use that expression. It exactly fitted her case, she felt that she was one of the castaways of the devil himself, and so she sought to tell of pardoning grace and dying love." You see, then, that Christ can save to the uttermost. Ah, it is so; it is so. If you have gone far into sin, weep over it; confess it before God with deep repentance, but come to Jesus Christ, just as you are; and, whoever you may be, there is no room for doubting. The door of the ark was a big door. There was room for the hare to go through, who went in quickly, and room for the snail to go through, with his slow pace; but there was plenty of room for the elephant when he came marching along; there was a chamber on purpose for him, and fodder on purpose for him. And so, ye elephantine sinners, there is a door big enough for you to come into the house of mercy; there is provision made, and a place for you; and without you the company will not be complete within the ark of saving grace.

May God bless that open declaration of the gospel to some poor devil's castaway who has got into a corner of the tabernacle to-night. May such be able to find hope too.

Well, now, I think I hear another say, "But I have a cause for doubt which has not yet been mentioned. I think I can guess it. *You doubt because you have so many times refused Christ, that you say you cannot expect him to receive you now.* That is the reason, is it not? "I have gone into great sin; sir," you say, or, "I have been trying to save myself by my self-righteousness and my good works. And I cannot expect him to receive me now." You think Christ is like the sons of men, such as you have known. Once a man went to a stable-keeper, and asked him what would be the price of a horse and gig for the day. "So much," he answered. "The enquirer went round the town to see if he could not get one cheaper, and when he found that he could not make a better bargain, he came back, and said that he would have the one which he had asked for at the first. "No," said the owner, "you will not. You have been going everywhere else, and now you may go where you have been. I do not want your custom." You fancy that Jesus Christ is like that, do you? You have been round to Moses and asked him the expense, and you find that you cannot meet the claims of the law; and you have been round to the pope, and asked him the price, and you find that ceremonies do not satisfy you. You have tried the Oxford way to heaven, and tried the Roman way to heaven, but they do not suit you. You cannot get there by them, and now you think you dare not come to Christ because you have so long neglected him. But you may come: he is willing to have you at any price. Nay, he is willing to have you at *no* price, and if you will come at no price—come without money and without price—he is still willing and able to receive you, for the gospel peals out yet these clarion notes, "Come and welcome! come and welcome! come and welcome! Whosoever will, let him take of the water of life freely!" O thou who doubtest Christ, wherefore dost thou doubt?

Now I will say no more but this. The way to deal with this state of mind of everlasting doubt and hesitation is to end it—to end it once for all. Repent, dear hearer, and may the Spirit of God help you to do so now. Repent of ever having disbelieved the Son of God. Repent of ever having distrusted the blood of Jesus Christ. Repent of ever having doubted the power of the omnipotent Spirit of God.

I know not to whom this word will come with power, but, in the name of Jesus Christ the Son of God, I command you to leave off doubting him, and to begin to believe in him at once. End your doubt without a moment's deliberation. You believe Christ Jesus to be God. I know you do. You believe what the Scripture saith concerning him—that he is a Saviour able to save. Man, by the living God I charge thee do not perpetrate such an insult to Christ as to go on doubting him. Thou hast the burden of all thy sin, but then he is a Saviour. Trust him with it; trust him now. "No," you say, "I will get home and pray." Do not wait for that. I wish you to pray when you get home, as much as ever you like; but, first of all, believe in Jesus Christ. Trust him on the spot. "Oh," says one, "it will be a venture." Venture, then, friend: venture. "May I pass in by the gate of mercy?" says another.

Pass through it, whether you may or not, for there never was a soul sent back for coming to Christ by mistake. Never was heard of such a thing as a soul attempting to pass in by the portal of faith, and Jesus Christ saying, "Ho, there! What are you at? You have no right to trust me. You are not one of my elect. You must go back, and you must not dare to trust me. You are not the kind of man I want." There was never such a case known, and there never will be such a case, for Christ's own words are, "Him that cometh to me I will in no wise cast out." That is, any "him" in all the world that comes to Christ he never will, he never can, cast out. I would make a dash for it, sinner, if I were you. Sink or swim, neck or nothing, here it is. I do believe—I must believe—in Jesus Christ; and, if I perish, still it shall be clinging to his cross. You will never perish there. May the Lord of covenant mercy draw you to this to-night, or drive you to it. I care not which, so long as you get to it, and Christ becomes all in all to your souls. Let us pray for that.

"Our Light Affliction"

"Our light affliction."—2 Corinthians iv. 17.

PERHAPS someone here thoughtlessly says, "Well, whoever calls affliction ' light ' must have been a person who knew very little about what affliction really is. If he had suffered as I have done, he would not have written about ' our light affliction.' He must have been in robust health, and known nothing of sickness and pain." "Just so," says another, " and if he had been as poor as I am, and had to work as hard as I do to maintain a sickly wife, and a large family, he would not have written about ' our light affliction.' I expect the gentleman who used that expression lived very much at his ease, and had all that his heart could wish." "Ay," says another, "and if he had stood by an open grave, and had to lament the loss of loved ones, as I have done, and if he had known what it was to be desolate and forsaken, as I have known it, he would not have written about ' our light affliction.' "

Now, if you do talk like that, you are all of you mistaken, for the man who wrote these words was probably afflicted more than any of us have ever been. The list of his afflictions that he gives us is perfectly appalling: "in stripes above measure, in prisons more frequent, in deaths oft. Thrice was I beaten with rods, once was I stoned, thrice I suffered shipwreck, a night and a day I have been in the deep; in journeyings often, in perils of waters, in perils of robbers, in perils by mine own countrymen, in perils by the heathen, in perils in the city, in perils in the wilderness, in perils in the sea, in perils among false brethren; in weariness and painfulness, in watchings often, in hunger and thirst, in fastings often, in cold and nakedness." Is there anyone here who could truthfully make out such a catalogue of personal afflictions as the apostle Paul endured?

"Well then," says one, "he must have been so hardened that he took no notice of it, like the Red Indian who will endure terrible torture without a groan, or like the Stoic philosopher who concealed his inward feelings beneath an unmoved countenance." No; you also are mistaken. If you read Paul's letters to his private friends and to the churches, you will see that they bear abundant evidences that he was a man of great tenderness of spirit and of intense emotion, one who could suffer and who did suffer most acutely. His education and training had fitted him for a life amongst the most learned and refined of his countrymen, yet he had so support himself by labouring as a tent-maker, and to journey hither and thither in peril and privation; and though he endured all this in absolute submission to the will of God, yet there was nothing stoical about his resignation.

"Well then," says another, "he must have been one of those care-less, light-hearted people who never trouble about anything that happens, and whose motto is, 'Let us eat and drink, for to-morrow we die.'" Oh, no! the apostle Paul was not at all that kind of man; he was the most thoughtful, logical, careful, considerate man of whom I have ever read. He knew what it was to be joyful, yet there was never any sign of levity about him. He had a grandly buoyant spirit which lifted him above waves of sorrow in which most men would have sunk, yet he was never frivolous. He wrote of "our light affliction" even when he was heavily afflicted, and while he acutely felt that affliction. The sailor forgets the storm when he is again safely on shore, and we are all apt to think less of our sickness when we have been restored from it; but Paul was in the midst of affliction when he called it "light." He felt the weight of it, and was fully conscious of the pressure of it upon his spirit; but the elastic spring of faith within his soul was so vigorously in action that he was enabled at that very time to call it "our light affliction."

We must not forget that Paul had afflictions which were peculiarly his own. There are afflictions which Christians have because they are Christians, and which those who are not Christians do not have; and Paul, as an apostle of Jesus Christ, had sufferings which were peculiarly his because he was an apostle. Because he was specially called to be the apostle of the Gentiles, because he was chosen to carry the gospel to many nations, because he was called to stand even before the cruel Emperor Nero,—for that very reason, he who was peculiarly gifted and specially chosen above all others to do most arduous and onerous work was also called to endure unusual trial. He had spelt out the word "AFFLICTION" as perhaps no other mere man had done, he had seen it written in capital letters across his whole life; so he could speak, not as a novice, but as one who had graduated in the school of affliction, and yet he wrote concerning "our light affliction." Before I have finished my discourse, I hope that most if not all here will agree with the apostle, and say, "We also call our affliction light."

I. I am going to speak, first, specially TO CHRISTIAN WORKERS; and to them I would say,—Dear brethren and sisters in Christ, *our affliction is light compared with the objects we have in view.*

Much of the affliction that the apostle had to endure came upon him because he was seeking the conversion of the heathen and the ingathering of the elect into the kingdom of Christ. If this is the object you also have in view, my dear friend, and you are made to suffer through your sedulous and faithful pursuit of it, I think you may truly call anything you have to endure a light affliction. If you have ever seen a mother sit up night after night with her sick child, you must have sometimes wondered that her eyes did not close in slumber. You were amazed that she did not permit someone else to share her task, but she seemed to think nothing of the cost to herself if she might only be the means of saving her little one's life. 'Twas love that made her labour light, and he who truly loves the souls of sinners will willingly bear any affliction for their sakes if he may but bring them to the Saviour. Yes, and he will also patiently endure affliction from them as he remembers how, in his own wilfulness and waywardness, he caused his Saviour to suffer on his behalf. If a man could know that, all through his life, he would have to wear a threadbare garment and exist upon very scanty fare; if he were sure that, throughout his life, he would meet with but little kindness from Christians, and with nothing but persecution from worldlings; and if, at the close of his career, he could only expect to be devoured by dogs or his body to be cast to the carrion crows, yet might he think all this to be but a light affliction if he might but win one soul from the unquenchable flame. Such trials as these are, happily, not necessary; but if they were, we might count them as nothing in comparison with the bliss of bringing up from the depths of sin the precious pearls that are for ever to adorn the crown of the Redeemer.

Still speaking to Christian workers, I have next to say that *our affliction is light compared with our great motive.*

What should be the great motive of all who seek to spread the gospel, and to win sinners for Christ? Surely there is no motive comparable to that of seeking to bring glory to God by gathering into the kingdom of Christ those for whom he shed his precious blood. Ever keep in memory, beloved, what Jesus has done for us. He left his radiant throne in glory, and condescended to take upon himself our nature, and also our sin,—

> "Bearing, that we might never bear,
> His Father's righteous ire."

Saved by his almighty grace, cleansed by his ever-precious blood, living because we have been made partakers of his life, how can we help loving him who has made us what we are? When that sacred passion burns vehemently within our hearts, we feel that any affliction that we have to endure in order to glorify Christ is too light to be even worth mentioning. O ye devoted lovers of the Saviour, have ye not known hours when ye have envied the martyrs, and wished that ye too might be allowed to wear the ruby crown? When you have read about how they had to lie for years in cold, damp dungeons, and then at last were dragged forth to die at the block, the stake, or the scaffold, have you not felt that your lives were poor and mean compared with theirs, and that you would gladly sacrifice all the comforts you now enjoy if you might be permitted to die for Christ as they did? I hope that many of you could truthfully say to your dear Lord and Saviour,—

> "Would not my ardent spirit vie
>   With angels round the throne,
> To execute thy sacred will,
>   And make thy glory known?

> "Would not my heart pour forth its blood
>   In honour of thy name,
> And challenge the cold hand of death
>   To damp the immortal flame?"

It was such a spirit as this that must have possessed the apostle Paul when he wrote concerning "our light affliction." Let us also, as workers for Christ, reckon as light affliction anything we have to endure by which we may glorify him who bore such a terrible weight of suffering and sorrow for us.

II. Now, secondly, I am going to speak TO THOSE WHO COMPLAIN OF THE WEIGHT OF THEIR AFFLICTION.

Dear brethren and sisters, let me remind you that *your affliction is light compared with that of many others.* Think of the horrors of a battlefield, and of the agonies of the poor wounded men who have to lie there so long untended. Living in peace in our happy island home, it is difficult for us to realize the misery and wretchedness that are being endured in Paris even while I am preaching to you.* Some of you complain of shortness of bread, but you have not to suffer the pangs of hunger as so many of the inhabitants of the French capital are at this moment suffering. There are some who are miserable as soon as any little ache or pain seizes them, yet their affliction is very light compared with that of many who never know what it is to be well and strong. Even if we are called to suffer pain, let us thank God that we have not been deprived of our reason. If we could go through the wards of Bethlehem Hospital, not far away from us, and see the many forms of madness

---

* It will be seen, from the date at the head of the Sermon, that it was preached during the Franco-Prussian war.

represented, I think each one of us would be moved to say, "My God, I thank thee that, however poor or sick I am, thou hast preserved me from such mental affliction as many have to bear." How thankful we all ought to be that we are not in prison! Does it seem improbable that such good people as we are could ever be numbered amongst the law-breakers of the land? You know how Hazael said to Elisha, "Is thy servant a dog, that he should do this great thing?" yet he did all that the prophet foretold; and but for the restraining grace of God, you and I, dear friends, might have been suffering the agony and remorse that many are to-night enduring in the prisons of this and other lands. I need not go on multiplying instances of those who are suffering in various ways in mind or body or estate; but I think I have said sufficient to convince you that our affliction, whatever form it may assume, is light compared with that of many others.

Next, *our affliction is light compared with our deserts.* We can truly say, with the psalmist, "He hath not dealt with us after our sins; nor rewarded us according to our iniquities." If the Lord had not dealt with us in mercy and in grace, we might have been at this moment beyond the reach of hope, like that rich man who in vain begged "Father Abraham" to send Lazarus to dip his finger in water to cool his parched tongue. Yes, ungodly one, you might have been in hell to-night, in that outer darkness where there is weeping and wailing and gnashing of teeth. Let the goodness of God in preserving you alive until now lead you to repent of your sin, and to trust in the Saviour. Thank God, you are still out of the pit; the iron gate has not yet been opened to admit you, and then been closed upon you for ever. Yet remember that you are, as it were, standing upon a narrow neck of land between two unbounded seas, and that the waves are every moment washing away the sand from beneath your feet, and rest no longer upon such an unsafe footing, lest it should give way altogether, and you should sink down into the fathomless abyss. As for any affliction that you ever can have to endure on earth, it is not merely light, it is absolutely unworthy of mention in comparison with the eternal woe that is the portion of the lost. Be thankful that, up to the present moment, this has not been your portion; and lest it should be, flee at once for refuge to lay hold upon the hope set before you in the gospel.

Then next, *our affliction is very light compared with that of our Lord.* Do you, dear friend, murmur at the bitterness of the draught in the cup which is put into your hand? But what heart can conceive of the bitterness of that cup of which Jesus drank? Yet he said, "The cup which my Father hath given me, shall I not drink it?" Is the disciple to be above his Master, and the servant above his Lord? Did Christ have to swim through stormy seas, and—

> "Must you be carried to the skies
> On flowery beds of ease?"

I think there is no consolation for an afflicted child of God so rich as that which arises from the contemplation of the sufferings of Jesus. The remembrance of the agony and bloody sweat of Gethsemane has often dried up the sweat of terror upon the anguished brow of the believer. The stripes of Jesus have often brought healing to his wounded followers. The thirst, the desertion, and the death on Golgotha—all the incidents of our Saviour's suffering, and the terrible climax of it all,—have been most helpful in assuaging the sorrows of stricken saints. Brethren and sisters in Christ, your sufferings are not worth a moment's thought when compared with the immeasurable agonies of Jesus your Redeemer. My soul would prostrate herself at his dear pierced feet, and say, "I have never seen any other affliction like thine affliction. I have beheld and seen, but I have never seen any sorrow like unto thy sorrow. Thou art indeed the incomparable Monarch of misery, the unapproachable King of the whole realm of grief. Of old, thou wert the 'Man of sorrows, and acquainted with grief,' and no man has ever been able to rob thee of thy peculiar title." I think that such reflections as these will help us to realize that, however heavy our affliction appears to us to be, it is very light compared with that of our dear Lord and Master.

> " Sons of God, in tribulation,
>   Let your eyes the Saviour view,
> He's the rock of our salvation,
>   He was tried and tempted too ;
>   All to succour
>   Every tempted, burden'd son."

And further, beloved, *our affliction is very light compared with the blessing which we enjoy.* Many of us have had our sins forgiven for Christ's sake, and the blessing of full and free forgiveness must far outweigh any affliction that we ever have to endure. When we were lying in the gloomy dungeon of conviction, and had not a single ray of hope to lighten the darkness, we thought that, even though we had to be kept in prison all our days, and to be fed only upon bread and water, we could be quite joyous if we could but be assured that God's righteous anger was turned away from us, and that our sins and iniquities he would remember against us no more for ever. Well, that is just what many of us have experienced; our transgressions have been forgiven, and our sin has been covered by the great atoning sacrifice of Jesus Christ our Lord and Saviour. Then let us rejoice and be glad all our days. But this is not all the blessing that we have received, for we have been clothed in the righteousness of Christ, and adopted into the family of God. Now we are heirs of God, and joint-heirs with Jesus Christ. We share even now in all the privileges of the children of God, and there are still greater favours and honours reserved for us in the future, as the apostle John saith, "Beloved, now are we the sons of God, and it doth not yet appear what we shall be ; but we know that, when

he shall appear, we shall be like him; for we shall see him as he is."
We already have a foretaste of the bliss that is laid up in store for
us, for—

> "The men of grace have found
> Glory begun below;
> Celestial fruits on earthly ground
> From faith and hope do grow."

So it is quite true that, in comparison with our blessings and
privileges, our affliction is indeed light.

And, dear friends, we specially realize that *our affliction is light
as we prove the power of the Lord's sustaining grace.* Some of you
have never personally proved its power, but many of you do know
by practical experience what I mean. There are times when,
through acute physical pain or great mental anguish, the soul is at
first utterly prostrate; but at last it falls back, in sheer helplessness,
upon the bosom of Jesus, gives up struggling, and resigns itself
absolutely to his will; and then—I speak what I do know, and
testify what I have felt,—there comes into the soul a great calm, a
quiet joy so deep and so pure as never is experienced at any other
time. I have sometimes looked back upon nights of pain,—pain so
excruciating that it has forced the tears from my eyes,—and I have
almost asked to have such suffering repeated if I might but have a
repetition of the seraphic bliss that I have often enjoyed under such
circumstances. I made a mistake when I said "seraphic" bliss, for
seraphs have not the capacity for suffering that we have, and therefore they can never experience that deep, intense, indescribable
bliss that is our portion when, by grace, we are enabled to glorify
God even in the furnace of affliction.

> "Let me but hear my Saviour say,
> 'Strength shall be equal to thy day!'
> Then I rejoice in deep distress,
> Leaning on all-sufficient grace.

> "I can do all things, or can bear
> All sufferings, if my Lord be there:
> Sweet pleasures mingle with the pains,
> While his left hand my head sustains."

We may well say that no affliction weighs more than a gnat resting
upon an elephant when the Lord's upholding grace is sweetly manifested to our soul in times of perplexity, anxiety, and pain. It is
just then that Jesus often so graciously reveals himself to us that we
even come to love the cross that brings him specially near to us.
I can understand that strange speech of Rutherford, as some have
regarded it, when he said that he sometimes feared lest he should
make his cross into an idol by loving affliction too much because of
the blessed results that flowed from it. The bark of the tree of
affliction may be bitter as gall; but if you get to the pith of it, you
will find that it is as sweet as honey.

Once more, affliction—*sanctified affliction becomes very light when we see to what it leads.* Sin is our great curse, and anything that can help to deliver us from the dominion of sin is a blessing to us. It seems that, in the constitution of our nature, and in the divine discipline under which we are being trained, our growth in grace is greatly assisted by affliction and trial. There are certain propensities to evil that can only be removed in the furnace, as the dross is burnt away from the pure metal; and surely, brethren, you who know the exceeding sinfulness of sin would not think any affliction too severe that should humble your pride, or subdue your passions, or slay your sloth, or overcome any other sin that so easily besets you. You will not merely acquiesce in the Lord's dealings with you, but you will devoutly thank him for using the sharp knife of affliction to separate you from your sin. A wise patient will gratefully thank the surgeon who cuts his flesh, and makes it bleed, and who will not allow it to heal up too quickly; and when God, by his gracious Spirit's operation, uses the stern surgery of trial to eradicate the propensity to sin, we do well to kiss the hand that holds the knife, and to say with cheerfulness as well as with resignation, "The will of the Lord be done."

> "It needs our hearts be wean'd from earth,
> It needs that we be driven,
> By loss of every earthly stay,
> To seek our joys in heaven."

Now, lastly, *our affliction is light compared with the glory which is so soon to be revealed to us and in us.* Some of us are much nearer to our heavenly home than we have ever imagined. Possibly, we are reckoning upon another twenty or even forty years of service, yet the shadows of our life's day are already lengthening although we are unaware that it is so. Perhaps we are anticipating long periods of fightings without and fears within, but those anticipations will never be realized, for the day of our final victory is close at hand, and then doubts and fears shall never again be able to assail our spirits. In this house to-night there may be some who are sitting on the very banks of the Jordan, and just across the river lies the land that floweth with milk and honey, the land which is reserved as the inheritance of the true children of God. Their eyes are so dimmed with tears that they cannot see—

> "Canaan's fair and happy land,
> Where their possessions lie."

They even imagine that they are captives by the waters of Babylon, and they hang their harps upon the willows, for they fear there are many years of banishment still before them. Yet the King's messenger is already on the way with the summons to bid them to appear before him very soon. Even if the call does not come to some of us at once, if the Master has need of us in this world a little longer, how soon our mortal life must end! What is our life? "It is even a vapour, that appeareth for a little time, and then vanisheth away." "As for man, his days are as grass; as a flower of the field, so he flourisheth. For the wind passeth over it, and it is gone; and the place thereof shall know it no more." But does the brevity of life cause us any anxiety? Oh, no! "For we know that if our earthly house of this tabernacle were dissolved, we have a building of God, a house not made with hands, eternal in the heavens;" and when once we reach that blest abode of all the saints, and look back upon our earthly experiences, we shall feel that any affliction we had to endure was light indeed compared with the unutterable bliss that shall then be our eternal portion. We are pilgrims to Zion's city bound, and we necessarily have certain privations and difficulties; but when our journey is at an end,—

> "One hour with our God
> Will make up for it all."

If we have not this good hope through grace, we may well say that our affliction is *not* light. I cannot imagine how any of you, my hearers, can go on living without a Saviour;—you poor people, you hard-working people, you sickly, consumptive people, how can you live without a Saviour? I wonder how those who are rich, and who have an abundance of earthly comforts, can live on year after year without any hope (except a false one) of comfort and blessing in the life that is to come. But as for you who have so few earthly comforts, you whose life is one long struggle for bare existence, you who scarcely know what it is to have a day without pain, how can *you* live without a Saviour? Remember that "godliness is profitable unto all things, having promise of the life that now is, and of that which is to come." So, "seek ye the Lord while he may be found, call ye upon him while he is near: let the wicked forsake his way, and the unrighteous man his thoughts: and let him return unto the Lord, and he will have mercy upon him; and to our God, for he will abundantly pardon." May the Lord give you the grace to come unto him this very moment, and to him shall be all the glory for ever, for Jesus Christ's sake. Amen.

The Pearl of Patience

"Ye have heard of the patience of Job, and have seen the end of the Lord; that the Lord is very pitiful, and of tender mercy."—James v. 11.*

WE need to be reminded of what we have *heard,* for we are far too ready to forget. We are also so slow to consider and meditate upon what we have heard that it is profitable to have our memories refreshed. At this time we are called upon to recollect that we have heard of the patience of Job. We have, however, I trust, gone beyond mere hearing, for we have also *seen* in the story of Job that which it was intended to set vividly before our mind's eye. "Ye have heard of the patience of Job, and have seen the end of the Lord." The Romish priest professes to make men hear the voice of the gospel by seeing, but the Scriptural way is to make men see the truth by hearing. Faith, which is the soul's sight, comes by hearing. The design of the preaching of the gospel to the ear is "to make all men see what is the fellowship of the mystery, which from the beginning of the world hath been hid in God, who created all things by Jesus Christ." Inward sight is the result of all fruitful hearing.

Now, that which is to be *seen* in the Scriptures is somewhat deeper, and calls for more thought than that which is merely heard. "Ye have heard of the patience of Job,"—an interesting history, which a child may understand; but it needs divine teaching to see to the bottom of that narrative, to discover the pearl which lies in the depths of it. It can only be said of enlightened disciples, "Ye have seen the end of the Lord; that the Lord is very pitiful, and of tender mercy." At the same time, that which is seen is also more precious to the heart, and more bountifully enriches the soul than anything which is only heard. I count it no small enrichment of our mind to have heard of the patience of Job, it comforts and strengthens us in our endurance; but it is an infinitely better thing to have seen the end of the Lord, and to have perceived the undeviating tenderness and pity which are displayed even in his sorest chastisements. This is indeed a choice vein of silver, and he that hath digged in it is far richer than the more superficial person, who has only heard of the patience of Job, and so has only gathered surface-truth. "The patience of Job," as we hear of it, is like the shell of some rare nut from the Spice Islands, full of fragrance; but "the end of the Lord," when we come to see it, is as the kernel, which is rich beyond expression with a fulness of aromatic essence.

Note well the reason why the text reminds us of what we have heard and seen. When we are called to the exercise of any great virtue, we need to call in all the helps which the Holy Spirit has bestowed upon us. All our wealth of hearing and seeing we shall have need to spend in our heavenly warfare. We shall be forced full often to gird up the loins of our mind by the recollection of examples of which we have heard, such as that of Job, and then to buckle up that girdle, and brace it fast with what we have seen. The patience of Job shall gird us, and that "end of the Lord" which we have seen shall be the fastening of the band. We shall need all ere our work is done. In the present case, the virtue we are called to exercise is that of *patience;* and therefore, to help us to do it, we are reminded of the things that we have heard and seen, because it is a grace as difficult as it is necessary, and as hard to come at as it is precious when it is gained.

The text is preceded by a triple exhortation to patience. In the seventh verse we read, "Be patient, therefore, brethren, unto the coming of the Lord;" and again, "Behold, the husbandman waiteth for the precious fruit of the earth, and hath long patience for it, until he receive the early and latter rain. Be ye also patient; stablish your hearts: for the coming of the Lord draweth nigh." Further on, in the tenth verse, we read, "Take my brethren, the prophets, who have spoken in the name of the Lord, for an example of suffering affliction, and of patience." Are we thrice exhorted to patience? Is it not clear that we have even now much need of it? We are most of us deficient in this excellent grace, and because of it we have missed many privileges, and have wasted many opportunities in which we might have honoured God, might have commended religion, and might have been exceedingly profited in our own souls. Affliction has been the fire which would have removed our dross, but impatience has robbed the mental metal of the flux of submission which would have secured its proper purification. It is unprofitable, dishonourable, weakening; it has never brought us gain, and never will.

1 suppose we are three times exhorted to patience because we shall need it much in the future. Between here and heaven we have no guarantee that the road will be easy, or that the sea will be glassy. We have no promise that we shall be kept, like flowers in a conservatory, from the breath of frost, or that, like fair queens, we shall be veiled from the heat of the sun.

The voice of wisdom saith, "Be patient, be patient, be patient; you may need a threefold measure of it; be ready for the trial." I suppose, also, that we are over and over again exhorted to be patient, because it is so high an attainment. It is no child's play to be dumb as the sheep before her shearers, and to lie still while the shears are taking away all that warmed and comforted us. The mute Christian under the afflicting rod is no every-day personage. We kick out like oxen which feel the goad for the first time; we are most of us for years as a bullock unaccustomed to the yoke. "Be patient, be patient, be patient," is the lesson to be repeated to our hearts many times, even as we have to teach children over and over again the selfsame words, till they know them by heart. It is the Holy Ghost, ever patient under our provocations, who calls us to be "patient." It is Jesus, the unmurmuring sacrifice, who charges us to "be patient." It is the long-suffering Father who bids us "be patient." O you who are soon to be in heaven, be patient for yet a little while, and your reward shall be revealed!

Upon these two things we will indulge a brief meditation. Firstly, we are bidden to be patient, and *it is not an unheard of virtue:* "Ye have heard of the patience of Job;" and, secondly, we are bidden to be patient, and *it is not an unreasonable virtue,* for ye "have seen the end of the Lord; that the Lord is very pitiful, and of tender mercy."

I. IT IS NOT AN UNHEARD OF VIRTUE TO BE PATIENT: "Ye have heard of the patience of Job."

Observe well that the patience of Job was the patience of *a man like ourselves,* imperfect and full of infirmity; for, as one has well remarked, we have heard of the impatience of Job as well as of his patience. I am glad the divine biographer was so impartial, for had not Job been somewhat impatient, we might have thought his patience to be altogether inimitable, and above the reach of ordinary men. The traces of imperfection which we see in Job prove all the more powerfully that grace can make grand examples out of common constitutions, and that keen feelings of indignation under injustice need not prevent a man's becoming a model of patience. I am thankful that I know that Job did speak somewhat bitterly, and proved himself a man, for now I know that it was a man like myself who said, "The Lord gave, and the Lord hath taken away; blessed be the name of the Lord." It was a man of flesh and blood, such as mine, who said, "Shall we receive good at the hand of God, and shall we not receive evil?" Yea, it was a man of like passions with myself who said, "Though he slay me, yet will I trust in him."

Ye have heard of the patience of your Lord and Master, and tried to copy it, and half despaired; but now ye have heard of the patience of his servant Job, and knowing as Job did that your Redeemer liveth, ye should be encouraged to emulate him in obedient submission to the will of the Lord.

"Ye have heard of the patience of Job," that is, the patience of *a greatly tried man*. That is a very trite yet needful remark: Job could not have exhibited patience if he had not endured trial; and he could not have displayed a patience whose fame rings down the ages, till we have heard of it, if he had not known extraordinary affliction. Reflect, then, that it was the patience of a man who was *tried in his estate*. All his wealth was taken! Two or three servants were left,—left only to bring him evil tidings, each one saying, "I only am escaped alone to tell thee." His flocks and his herds were gone, the house in which his children had met was a wreck, and the princely man of Uz sat upon a dunghill, and there were none so mean as to do him reverence. Ye have heard of the patience of Job in loss and poverty; have ye not seen that, if all estates should fail, God is your portion still?

Job was caused to suffer sharp *relative troubles*. All his children were snatched away without a warning, dying at a festival, where, without being culpably wrong, men are usually unguarded, and in a sense unready, for the spirit is in *déshabille*. His children died suddenly, and there was a grievous mystery about it, for a strange wind from the wilderness smote the four corners of the house, and overthrew it in an instant; and such an occurrence must have connected itself in Job's mind either with the judgment of God or with Satanic influence,—a connection full of the most painful thoughts and surmises. The death of his dear ones was not a common or a desirable one, and yet all had so been taken. Not a son or daughter was left him. All gone! All gone! He sits among the ashes a childless man. "Ye have heard of the patience of Job." Oh, to have patience under bereavements, patience even when the insatiate archer multiplies his arrows!

Then, and I here speak most to myself, "Ye have heard of the patience of Job" under *personal affliction*. It is well said by one who knew mankind cruelly well, that "we bear the afflictions of other people very easily;" but when it touches our bone and our flesh, trial assumes an earnest form, and we have need of unusual patience. Such bitter pain as Job must have suffered, we have probably none of us known to anything like the same degree: and yet we have had weary nights and dreary days. Each limb has claimed a prominence in anguish, and each nerve has become a road for armies of pains to march over. We know what it is to feel thankful tears in our eyes merely for having been turned over in bed. Job, however, far excels us. "Ye have heard of the patience of Job," and ye know how he sinned not when from the crown of his head to the sole of his foot he was covered with irritating boils.

In addition to all this, Job bore what is perhaps the worst form of trial, namely, *mental distress.* The conduct of his wife must have much grieved him when she tempted him to "curse God, and die." However she meant it, or however her words may be translated, she evidently spoke like a foolish woman when her husband needed wise consolation. And then those "miserable comforters", how they crowned the edifice of his misery! Cold-blooded mortals sneer at sentimental grievances, but I speak from my heart when I affirm that griefs which break no bones and take not a groat from our store may yet be among the sharpest whips of sorrow. When the iron enters into the soul, we know the very soul of suffering. See how Job's friends fretted him with arguments, and worried him with accusations. They rubbed salt into his wounds, they cast dust into his eyes, their tender mercies were cruel, though well-intentioned. Woe to the man who in his midnight hour is hooted at by such owls; yet the hero of patience sinned not. "Ye have heard of the patience of Job."

Job's was in all respects a most real trouble, he was no mere dyspeptic, no hysterical inventor of imaginary evil; his were no fancied losses nor minor calamities. He had not lost one child out of a numerous family, nor a few thousands out of a vast fortune, but he was brought to sad bereavement, abject poverty, and terrible torment of body and mind; but, despite it all, "Ye have heard of the patience of Job," and heard more of his patience than of his afflictions. What a mercy to have heard of such a man, and to know that one of our own race passed through the seven-times-heated furnace, and yet was not consumed!

The patience of Job was the patience of *a man who endured up to the very end.* No break-down occurred; at every stage he triumphed, and to the utmost point he was victorious. Traces of weakness are manifest, but they are grandly overlaid by evidences of gracious power. What a marvellous man was he with all those aches and pains, still bearing witness to his God, "But he knoweth the way that I take: when he hath tried me, I shall come forth as gold." He reasons well even in the heat of his passionate zeal for his character; he reasons bravely too, and catches up the points of his adversaries like a trained logician. He holds fast his integrity, and will not let it go; and best of all, he cries, "I know that my Redeemer liveth, and that he shall stand at the latter day upon the earth: and though after my skin worms destroy this body, yet in my flesh shall I see God." Oh, glorious challenge of a dying man to his immortal Kinsman!

The enemy could not triumph over Job; he threw him on a dunghill, and it became his throne, more glorious than the ivory throne of Solomon. The boils and blains with which the adversary covered the patriarch were more honour to him than a warrior's gilded corslet. Never was the arch-fiend more thoroughly worsted than by the afflicted patriarch; and instead of pitying the sufferer, my pity curdles into contempt for that fallen spirit who must there have gnawed his own heart, and drunk deep draughts of gall and wormwood as he saw himself foiled at all points by one who had been put into his power, and one too of the feeble race of man. Surely, in this he experienced a foretaste of the bruising threatened at Eden's gate as to be given him by the woman's seed. Yes, Job endured unto the end, and hence he stands as a pillar in the house of the Lord. Cannot we endure unto the end too? What doth hinder grace from glorifying itself in us?

We may once more say that the patience of Job is the virtue of *one who thereby has become a great power for good*. "*Ye* have heard of the patience of Job;" yes, and all the ages have heard of the patience of Job, and heaven has heard of the patience of Job, and hell has heard of it too; and not without results in each of the three worlds. Among men, the patience of Job is a great moral and spiritual force. This morning, when musing upon it, I felt ashamed and humbled, as thousands have done before me. I asked myself, "What do I know of patience when I compare myself with Job?" and I felt that I was as unlike the great patriarch as I well could be. I recollect a minister who had been somewhat angered by certain of his people, and therefore preached from the text, "And Aaron held his peace." It was remarked that the preacher's likeness to Aaron reached no further than the fact that Aaron held his peace, and the preacher did not. May we not penitently confess that our likeness to Job is much of the same order: he was patient, and we are not? Yet, as I thought of the patience of Job, it caused me to hope. If Job was patient under trial and affliction, why should not I be patient too? He was but a man; what was wrought in one man may be done in another. He had God to help him, and so have I; he could fall back upon the living Redeemer, so can I; and why should I not? Why should not I attain to patience as well as the man of Uz? It made me feel happy to believe in human capacity to endure the will of God, the Holy Spirit instructing and upholding. Play the man, beloved friend! Be not cast down! What God hath done for one he can do for another. If the man be the same, and if the great God be the same, and be sure he is, we too may attain to patience in our limited circle; our patience may be heard of among those who prize the fruits of the Spirit.

II. I will not detain you, lest I weary you, except just to say, in the second place, IT IS NOT AN UNREASONABLE VIRTUE TO BE PATIENT, for, according to our text, there is great love and tenderness in it, "Ye have seen the end of the Lord; that the Lord is very pitiful, and of tender mercy."

We must have seen, in Job's story, if we have regarded it aright, that *the Lord was in it all*. It is not a narrative in which the devil is the sole actor, the great Lord of all is evidently present. He it was who challenged Satan to consider Job, and then questioned him as to the result. Less seen than the evil one, the Lord was nevertheless present at every act of the drama. God was not away while his servant suffered; in fact, if there was any place where the thoughts of God were centred more than anywhere else in providence at that time, it was where the perfect and upright man was bearing the brunt of the storm. *The Lord was ruling too.* He was not present as a mere spectator, but as still master of the situation. He had not handed over the reins to Satan; far from it, for every step that the enemy took was only by express permission from the throne. He allowed him to strip his servant, but he set the limit, "Only upon himself put not forth thine hand." When to complete the test the enemy was permitted to plague his body, the Lord added, "But save his life." The ruling hand is always on the curb. The dog of hell is allowed to snap and snarl, but his chain is not removed, and the collar of omnipotent restraint is on him. Come, dear friends, you that are in trouble, remember that God is in your sorrow, ruling it to a desired end, and checking it that it should go no further than according to his will; and you neither have suffered, nor in the future will suffer, any more than he in infinite love permits.

Moreover, *the Lord was blessing Job by all his tribulation.* Untold blessings were coming to the grand old man while he seemed to be losing all. It was not simply that he obtained a double portion at the end; but, all along, every part of the testing process wrought out his highest good. Now have we seen the end of the Lord, and that end is unmingled goodness. The Lord was standing by every moment to stop the refining process when it had come to the proper point, so that no more of it should happen than was really beneficial, and at the same time no less than should secure his gracious purpose. True mercy is bound at times to seem untender, for it might be a great and lifelong evil for the surgeon to stop the knife before its work was done: the Lord was wisely tender and tenderly wise with Job, and even in his case the sore affliction was not allowed to proceed a single degree beyond the needful point of intensity.

And when we come to look all Job's life through, we see that *the Lord in mercy brought him out of it all with unspeakable advantage.* He who tested with one hand supported with the other. Whatever Satan's end might be in tempting the patriarch, God had an end which covered and compassed that of the destroyer, and that end was answered all along the line, from the first loss which happened among the oxen to the last taunt of his three accusers. There was never a question in the heights of heaven as to the ultimate issue. Eternal mercy was putting forth its irresistible energy, and Job was made to bear up through the trial, and to rise from it a wiser and a better man.

Such is the case with all afflicted saints. We may well be patient under our trials, for the Lord sends them; he is ruling in all their circumstances, he is blessing us by them, he is waiting to end them, and he is pledged to bring us through. Shall we not gladly submit to the Father of our spirits? Is not this our deepest wish, "Thy will be done"? Shall we quarrel with that which blesses us? Shall we repine when the end of the trouble is so near and so blessed? No; we see that the Lord is very pitiful and of tender mercy, and therefore we will be patient.

Beloved, let us accept future sorrow with joy, for it is love divine which will add to our years whatever sorrowful seasons may yet come to us. Job's life might have ended in the first period without the trial; but if the patriarch, with perfect knowledge of all things, could have had his choice, would he not have chosen to endure the trial for the sake of all the blessing which came of it? We should never have heard of the patience of Job if he had continued in his prosperity; and that first part of his life would have made a very poor commonplace history as compared with what we now find in the pages of Scripture. Camels, sheep, servants, and children make up a picture of wealth, but we can see this any day; the rare sight is the patience, this it is which raises Job to his true glory. God was dealing well with his faithful servant, and even rewarding his uprightness, when he counted him worthy to be tried. The Lord was taking the surest and kindest way to bless and honour one who was a perfect and an upright man, one that feared God, and eschewed evil.

It was pitiful of the Lord to permit sharp trial to come upon Job for his good; there was more tender mercy in subjecting him to it than there would have been in screening him from it. False pity would have permitted the good man to die in his nest, but true pity put a thorn into it, and made him mount aloft as the eagle. It was great mercy, after all, which took him out of the state in which he washed his steps with butter, and cast him into the mire, for thus he was weaned from the world, and made to look the more eagerly for a better portion.

No doubt, in Job's character, the Lord saw certain failings which we cannot see, which he desired to remove, and perhaps he also marked some touches of grace which needed to be supplied; and divine love undertook to complete his perfect character. Perhaps his prosperity had sunned him till he had grown somewhat hard in tone and sharp in judgment, and therefore the Lord would soften down and mellow his gracious spirit. The things lacking were no common virtues, for in these he was perfect, but certain rich and rare tints of the higher life; and these could not be imparted by any other means than severe suffering. Nothing more could really be done for Job but by this special agency, for doubling the number of his camels and sheep would only enlarge his cares, since he had enough already; of children, too, he had a sufficient family, and of all earthly things abundance; but to give him twice the grace, twice the experience, twice the knowledge of God, perhaps twice the tenderness of character he had ever possessed before, was a mode of enrichment which the tender and pitiful Lord adopted out of the greatness of his wisdom and favour. Job could only thus be made doubly rich in the rarest of all treasures, and the All-merciful adopted that method.

Examining the matter from another point of view, it may appear that Job was tried in order that he might be better able to bear the extraordinary prosperity which the Lord had resolved to pour in upon him. That double portion might have been too much for the patriarch if he had not been lifted into a higher state. If abundance be hard to bear, superfluity is even worse; and, therefore, to those he loves, the Lord giveth more grace.

Job by his trials and patience received not only double grace, and double wealth, but double honour from God. He had stood very high in the peerage of the excellent as a perfect and an upright man before his trial, but now he is advanced to the very highest rank of spiritual nobility. Even our children call him "the most patient man under pains and sufferings." He rose from the knighthood of sincere goodness to the peerage of heroic endurance. At first, he had the honour of behaving admirably amid wealth and ease, but he was in the end elevated to sit among those who glorify God in the fires. Benevolence, justice, and truth shone as bright stars in the sky of his heavenly character, but now the moon of patience silvers all, and lights up the scene with a superior beauty. Perhaps the Lord may love some of us so specially that he means to put upon us the dignity of endurance, he will make us knights, not of the golden fleece, but of the iron cross. What but great pitifulness and tender mercy could plan such a lot for our unworthy selves?

Once more, Job by his trials and the grace of God was lifted up into the highest position of usefulness. He was useful before his trial as few men of wealth and influence have been, but now his life possesses an enduring fruitfulness which blesses multitudes every day. Even we who are here this afternoon "have heard of the patience of Job." All the ages have this man for their teacher. Brothers and sisters, we do not know who will be blessed by our pains, by our bereavements, by our crosses, if we have patience under them. Specially is this the case with God's ministers, if he means to make much of them: their path to usefulness is up the craggy mountain's side. If we are to comfort God's afflicted people, we must first be afflicted ourselves. Tribulation will make our wheat fit to be bread for saints. Adversity is the choicest book in our library, printed in black letter, but grandly illuminated. Job makes a glorious comforter and preacher of patience, but no one turns either to Bildad, Zophar, or Eliphaz, who were "miserable comforters" because they had never been miserable. You, dear sisters, whom God will make daughters of consolation to your families, must in your measure pass through a scholarship of suffering too; a sword must pass through your own hearts if you are to be highly favoured and blessed among women. Yet, let us all remember that affliction will not bless us if it be impatiently borne; if we kick at the goad, it will hurt us, but it will not act as a fitting stimulus. If we rebel against God's dispensations, we may turn his medicines into poisons, and increase our griefs by refusing to endure them. Be patient, be patient, be patient, and the dark cloud shall drop a sparkling shower. "Ye have heard of the patience of Job:" imitate it. "Ye have seen the end of the Lord:" rejoice in it. "He is very pitiful, and of tender mercy:" yield yourselves to him. Divine Spirit, plant in us the sweet flower of patience, for our patient Saviour's sake! Amen.